The Complete
Leader's Companion to
The JGirl's Guide:
The Young Jewish Woman's
Handbook for Coming of Age
by Penina Adelman,
Ali Feldman and
Shulamit Reinharz

THE J Girl's
Teacher's and Parent's
Guide

Miriam P. Polis

with Shulamit Reinharz

Miriam P. Polis has been a Jewish educator for over twenty years. She runs Panim el Panim Consulting, a Jewish educational consulting service specializing in the integration of science, music, and the arts with the study of Tanach and Talmud. For further information contact her at mpolis@gmail.com.

The JGirl's Guide Teacher's and Parent's Guide
© 2005 by The Hadassah–Brandeis Institute

For information regarding permission to reprint material from this book, please mail or fax your request in writing to Jewish Lights Publishing, Permissions Department, at the address / fax number listed below, or send an e-mail to permissions@jewishlights.com.

ISBN 1-58023-225-6

Manufactured in the United States of America

Published by Jewish Lights Publishing
A Division of LongHill Partners, Inc.
Sunset Farm Offices, Route 4, P.O. Box 237
Woodstock, VT 05091
Tel: (802) 457-4000   Fax: (802) 457-4004
www.jewishlights.com

CONTENTS

ACKNOWLEDGMENTS

Because I have worked in the field of Jewish education for over twenty years, I have had the opportunity to spend time with preteen and teenage girls in formal and casual settings. During those years it was challenging to find a book that spoke to their experiences. I would so much have liked to have had a resource that addressed the needs and real questions of bat mitzvah–age girls. Therefore, when the Hadassah-Brandeis Institute staff invited me to read some selected chapters from *The JGirl's Guide* for the purpose of writing a leader's guide for teachers and parents, I knew this was a project for me.

I am grateful to הקב"ה for permitting me to use my gifts and experience to write this guide. It is my hope that teachers and parents will find the book helpful as they foster the next generation of strong Jewish women. More than that, I hope those who read this book will be inspired to go beyond what I've written and will use it as a foundation to enrich their students' or children's learning.

Nothing of value is ever produced without the help, guidance, and support of many people and this book is no exception. It is with deep הכרת הטוב that I thank the following individuals:

Edith (Edie) Querido of Baltimore, who funded the preparation of this guide.

Nancy Vineberg, director of communications and strategic planning of the Hadassah-Brandeis Institute, for recruiting me.

Shulamit Reinharz, director of the Hadassah-Brandeis Institute, for choosing me to undertake this wonderful endeavor and working with me to craft each chapter. Ali Feldman and Penina Adelman for writing *The JGirl's Guide* with Shula and for making invaluable suggestions.

Clare Murphy, children's library assistant at the Brookline Public Library, was of invaluable assistance providing sources and encouraging e-mails.

Risa Krohn and everyone at the Israel Book Store for enthusiastically providing me with sources and assistance.

Leah Summers, friend, colleague, and superb Jewish educator, for helping me cross the finish line.

Lydia Levis Bloch of Baltimore, dear friend, for giving me suggestions for the lesson "Eating."

Lyuda Packer, Julia Packer, and Tamara Packer for sharing their thoughts as thirteen- and twelve-year-old girls, and their mother, Judy Packer, for coordinating schedules until we could find a time to talk!

Rabbi Gershon Gewirtz, my rabbi, for tracking down citations based only on, "I remember learning this years ago…. Could it be in a Gemara?"

Rochelle Perman, Amy Farber, and Mimi Feuerstein for their loving support and for beginning every conversation with the words, "How's the guide coming?"

אחרון אחרון חביב, the last is the dearest. This guide is dedicated to Neil. נר ה' נשמת אדם Hashem's lamp is not the only lamp lit by your soul.

INTRODUCTION

When I was fourteen years old I had my first taste of teaching in a "formal" setting. I was in charge of the arts and crafts program at a local Jewish camp. I still remember the excitement of planning projects, the delight of working with the kids, and the joy of doing creative work for the Jewish people. That summer led me to my first teaching job. I was hooked! Since then I've taught kindergarten through twelfth grade in Jewish day schools and afternoon schools, students and teachers, children and adults. I became a teacher because I love to learn and I cherish the sense of awe and wonderment I see in my students' faces with each new discovery.

The JGirl's Guide speaks directly to young women. This leader's guide is for teachers and parents using *The JGirl's Guide* with their students or children. *The JGirl's Guide* offers tools to help preteen and early teen girls deal with their current concerns using Jewish ideas. I hope it will help you show girls that their heritage can guide them as they grow up.

This is a tall order for such a small book! However, I believe the goal is achievable one mitzvah at a time. Each chapter in *The JGirl's Guide* presents at least one mitzvah and uses it as the chapter's focus. This guide offers ideas for helping the girls understand what bat mitzvah actually means: becoming a female who understands what mitzvot are and can carry them out—a Jewish girl who both knows and does.

Each chapter of *The JGirl's Guide* stands on its own. Thus, *it is not necessary to read the chapters in order or even to cover every chapter.* As with any good teaching, much will depend upon the group of girls with whom you are working, who they are as individuals and how they hang together as a group. Moreover, *The JGirl's Guide is not only for the bat mitzvah–age girl, but can be used with girls of almost any age.*

Throughout this leader's guide I frequently refer to God. I write about girls doing things with God and for God, and God doing things for the girls. Teachers and parents should recognize that the girls may wish to engage in conversation about God. I do not make the assumption that all the girls believe in God. I do assume that they have questions. The purpose of this guide is not to push girls onto a particular path; its purpose is to open lines of communication and inquiry. This is just one of many challenging components in dealing with the bat mitzvah–age girl.

It was my intention to produce lessons in an easy-to-read format that is consistent from lesson to lesson. Each one begins by listing the **Mitzvah** or **Mitzvot** covered in the corresponding chapter and also in the lesson. Specific **Goals** are listed for the lesson, followed by **Texts**. The **Texts** are usually incorporated into the lesson, but might also just be tools for the leader to consider *in addition* to the lesson. Whenever I taught middle school, Torah, or Rabbinic classes I always posted a quote or question on the board for my students to ponder. These quotes helped frame the content of the lesson. The **Texts** in this guide may be used in a similar manner. The **Quotes** that appear in the lessons come from *The JGirl's Guide* and will help the leader and girls connect with the material in each chapter.

In *Mishnah Avot* 2:20 Rabbi Tarfon says, "The day is short, the task is great." I know how much time and energy each teacher puts into creating lessons. To help you save time, I have tried to anticipate what will need to be prepared in advance and have listed that in the section entitled **Preparation**. The **Body of the Lesson** is written in a friendly style. Through my work as a mentor of teachers I know that there is a wide range of comfort level and experience out in the field. In the **Body of the Lesson** I usually offer a suggested "script." It is just a suggestion. My hope is that my words will spark your own creative ideas, producing an even richer lesson than what you find here.

Because girls around bat mitzvah age are reading more, thinking more, and processing more information than they did in their younger years, I wanted them to have a chance to build their vocabularies. Using words clearly will enable them to communicate in a more sophisticated manner. I have therefore included a **Dictionary Definitions** section. Sometimes the words are pulled from the given chapter. At other times I've simply included words I think relate to the subject at hand. All definitions come from *Webster's New Universal Unabridged Dictionary* (Avenel, NJ: Barnes & Noble Books, 1989).

As Jews we have a beautiful language in which our holy texts and liturgy are written—Hebrew. I believe it's important to expose students to as much Hebrew as possible. On the other hand, I realize many American Jews today may know very little Hebrew. Teachers and parents can serve as role models, learning together with the students. Thus, I strongly encourage the leader to use Hebrew words as often as possible. Because certain ideas can be communicated only through the Hebrew language, it is important to have these key words at your fingertips. Think about Yiddish words that you know, such as "schlep" and "chutzpah." Could you define them? It's tough because they have layers of meaning and have even acquired a place in the English language! The **Hebrew Words and Their Roots** section is designed to give the leader opportunities to use Hebrew phrases and enrich the girls' vocabularies. In the very first lesson the leader may wish to say a few words about the special quality of the Hebrew language. The fact that שרשים (root words) are at the core of the Hebrew language is important for the leader to point out to the girls: a שרש can be seen in many different forms. (See for example the words שכן, שכנה, and משכן in Lesson 1, "Being a Friend.")

There are many ways to utilize the **Hebrew Words and Their Roots** section. Here are a few suggestions:

- The leader should strive to use the Hebrew words in regular conversation as often as possible. The more frequently the girls hear the words, the more likely they will be to internalize the meanings and make the words their own.

- Because there are many different modes of learning, for the visual learner it will be helpful to see the words as well as hear them. As each lesson opens the leader can have the Hebrew word and a pictorial depiction of the word on a large card. The words can then be placed in strategic places around the room.

- Another way for the girls to "own" the vocabulary is to have them use the words in their journal, their יומן (see below). For example, לשון הרע is an important Hebrew phrase and concept. Writing and using a phrase such as לָשׁוֹן הָרַע in their journals offers the girls an opportunity to explore concepts and ideas while also establishing a personal connection to the vocabulary.

To be Jewish is to ask questions. It is through our questions that we refine our thinking and explore new avenues of inquiry. I have included a section entitled **Challenging Questions the Teacher May Want to Raise; Or the Girls May Raise** with two purposes in mind. First is to prepare the leader for some of the questions the girls might ask. Some of these questions come from my own experience with this age group, some directly from teenage girls themselves. Second, as the leader, you may wish to ask some of these questions of the girls to stimulate discussion. Letting the girls know you enjoy dealing with their challenging questions will create a secure environment open to all ideas.

Being reflective is an important part of maturation. There are many opportunities for reflection in each lesson. The **Challenging Questions the Teacher May Want to Raise; Or the Girls May Raise** is set up to engage the girls by utilizing different modes of learning: *chevruta* (a learning pair), small group discussion, whole-group discussion, and journaling. Regarding journaling, I suggest that the leader provide an opportunity for each girl to create a journal that she will use beginning with the first lesson. I would call the journal a יוֹמָן. (Explain to the girls that this word has as its שׁוֹרֶשׁ the word יוֹם, "day," giving you the chance to emphasize that contemplation should be a daily process.) Each girl can create a cover page that reflects their personality, interests, dreams, and the like. An opportunity can be created after or during each lesson for the girls to reflect on their experience and use the Hebrew vocabulary they are learning (see above).

The **Things to Think About** section is designed to put a חֲתִימָה, a seal, on the lesson. It's meant to help the leader achieve some closure on the chapter, though, truth be told, each chapter raises issues that can continue for a lifetime! **Other Sources** is my attempt to provide you and the girls with additional resources—books, music, and movies—for further study. I'm sure you will have others of your own.

You will note that at the end of *The JGirl's Guide* there are several small sections: "Glossary," "About the Jewish Religious Movements," "For More Information…," "Notes," "My Thoughts," and "Books Published by Jewish Lights." I encourage you to read each of these sections before using *The JGirl's Guide* with the girls, as they are sources for you and will help create a richer experience.

The "Glossary" section has Hebrew words and phrases (in transliteration) that are used throughout *The JGirl's Guide*. It would be helpful to read the Glossary before using the book.

"About the Jewish Religious Movements" was placed in *The JGirl's Guide* to provide a brief synopsis of the movements. Obviously, there are *many other* Jewish movements, such as Chabad, Jewish Renewal, and Chavurah. To reduce the complications in naming all the movements, the authors of *The JGirl's Guide* decided to include only the four major movements—Reform, Reconstructionist, Conservative, and Orthodox Judaism.

In addition to these religious movements, there are many other ways people choose to identify as Jews. Many Jews are unaffiliated with any particular movement, but strongly identify as Jews. Others consider themselves to be secular Jews or cultural Jews. It is important for the leader to be respectful of all types of Jews and share that respect with the girls. Some girls will decide *if* they will be Jewish as a teenager because that decision has been left up to them. It's recommended that the leader communicate to the girls that everyone is on a journey as a Jew and as a person, and that this is a lifelong voyage.

"For More Information" provides resources by category. The leader may wish to look through the list and utilize some of the sources in the lessons. While the list is by no means exhaustive, it does provide an excellent place to begin.

"Notes" are the endnotes for each chapter. Often readers ignore endnotes; however, I strongly encourage the leader to look up the endnotes. This will supply the leader with additional information and greater knowledge.

"My Thoughts" are blank pages to allow the process of reflection to begin, and "Books Published by Jewish Lights" gives the leader additional resources to investigate.

The JGirl's Guide is designed for a girl to read *on her own* or *with her parents*. This leader's guide is to help teachers or parents use *The JGirl's Guide* in a group format, to bring about new levels of learning beyond that of an individual or two people. Although this leader's guide was written with teachers in mind and addresses them in the lessons, parents are the ultimate teachers (there's only the difference of one letter in Hebrew between the words "teacher" and "parent"). Thus parents, too, are invited to use the leader's guide to enrich their daughters' experience.

You will notice that the chapters in *The JGirl's Guide* are all written in the active tense—resting, eating, being a friend, and others. Before beginning the first lesson I would recommend spending some time with the girls examining the Table of Contents and discussing why the chapter titles are written in this manner. A former colleague and mentor, Audrey Goldfarb, used to have a small sign on her office door that read, "We are human beings, not human doings." My first day on the job Audrey told me she had that sign up to remind her every day that we are defined by process, not by product. This might be an interesting saying to discuss with the girls in light of the chapter titles.

I end this introduction with a quote from one of my very favorite songs, a Chanukah song. The opening words are:

"בָּנוּ חֹשֶׁךְ לְגָרֵשׁ, בְּיָדֵנוּ אוֹר וָאֵשׁ. כָּל אֶחָד הוּא אוֹר קָטֹן, וְכֻלָּנוּ אוֹר אֵיתָן."

"Come, let us banish the darkness. In our hands are light and fire. Each one of us is a small light, [but] together we are a powerful, strong light."

This leader's guide is but a small light, but in your hands may it become a powerful, strong light that will help our girls grow as individuals, as leaders and as members of a vibrant Jewish community.

MIRIAM P. POLIS

BEING A FRIEND

MITZVOT

ואהבת לרעך כמוך *Ve'ahavta l'reyakha kamokha* (love your neighbor as yourself); גמילות חסדים *G'milut chasadim* (acts of lovingkindness)

GOALS

To explore the definition of friendship given on p. 2 of *The JGirl's Guide.*

To identify גמילות חסדים, *g'milut chasadim* in one's self and in one's friends.

To encourage reflection on the difference between *being* a friend and *making* a friend.

TEXTS/QUOTES

ואהבת לרעך כמוך *Ve'ahavta l'reyakha kamokha*—love your neighbor as yourself (Leviticus 19:18).

"People define friendship differently, but all definitions have certain things in common: trust, loyalty, care, respect, understanding, similar values and shared interests, enjoying time together, and feeling comfortable around each other" (*The JGirl's Guide,* p. 2).

גמילות חסדים *G'milut chasadim*—acts of lovingkindness.

David and Jonathan: "They were called good friends because they loved each other and would have done anything for one another" (*The JGirl's Guide,* p. 5).

Ruth and Naomi: Ruth is a model for גמילות חסדים, *g'milut chasadim.* "The world rests on three things: Torah, service to God, and acts of lovingkindness" (*Pirkei Avot* 1:2).

PREPARATION

Students should read Chapter 1 of *The JGirl's Guide,* "Being a Friend." Have students complete the first paragraph under "Do It" on p. 4. (Teachers, note that on a given day a student may feel she doesn't have *any* friends! Offer her the option of writing the 10 points about herself.)

Remember that the יומן should be introduced in this lesson. (See Introduction.)

ROOM PREPARATION

Arrange chairs/desks in a manner that allows each girl to be visible to all of her classmates. Have large sheets of paper set up on the board (or if you use an overhead, have blank overhead transparencies available).

BODY OF LESSON

Share with the girls that *The JGirl's Guide* begins with two very important concepts in Judaism. Over the generations people have tried to articulate the most important Jewish value. In the famous story of Hillel and Shammai and the convert (*Shabbat* 31a), Hillel tells the convert, "[The whole Torah can be distilled down to:] Don't do onto others what is hateful to you. All the rest is commentary. Now go and learn!" Ask the girls if they agree with Hillel's assessment of Torah. Does גמילות חסדים, *g'milut chasadim,* embody the same idea as Hillel's response? Although the Ten Commandments deal with how we need to treat one another, friendship isn't specifically mentioned. Ask the girls why they think this idea is absent.

Discuss with the girls that the two examples of friendship given here—between David and Jonathan, and Ruth and Naomi—are extraordinary ones. The individuals are adults, not young people. Do they think adult friendships are different than young people's friendships? If so, how? How far does one have to go to be a friend? Are there degrees of friendship? We sometimes say, "She's my best friend." Is that different from someone we hang out with somewhat regularly? What might be an example of extraordinary friendship in modern times? Does everyone we're friends with have to be an extraordinary friend?

Teacher: "You've read the chapter 'Being a Friend.' Today you're going to have an opportunity to explore what it means to be a friend and how גמילות חסדים, *g'milut chasadim,* shapes that idea. Let's start by sharing what you thought was most important about your friends. You've all written 10 points about your friend. I'd like to post two points from every girl's list. Share with us things that might be unique to your friend."

After all the points are written on the board/overhead, "Take the next few minutes to look at the points we've listed on the board and this quote from the book I've posted on the wall: 'People define friendship differently, but all definitions have certain things in common: trust, loyalty, care, respect, understanding, similar values and shared interests, enjoying time together, and feeling comfortable around each other' (*The JGirl's Guide*, p. 2). Sit with another girl in the room and discuss this definition. Some possible questions to explore are: (1) Are there any points on the board that connect to the definition? (2) Do we agree with this definition? Is there anything we'd add/subtract? (3) According to this definition, am I a good friend? (4) How could thinking about the ideas on the list and in the definition help me to be a better friend?

"You've already read the stories of David and Jonathan, and Ruth and Naomi. Both Jonathan and Ruth showed extraordinary גמילות חסדים, *g'milut chasadim,* to David and Naomi. The Rabbis in *Pirkei Avot* tell us: 'The world rests on three things: Torah, service to God, and acts of lovingkindness' (*Pirkei Avot* 1:2)—על שלשה דברים העולם עומד על התורה ועל העבודה ועל גמילות חסדים. For the next fifteen minutes we're going to prepare a game. We'll work in groups of four. Each group will be given a stack of 3" x 5" cards. You'll be writing on both sides of the card. On one side write an example of גמילות חסדים, *g'milut chasadim,* such as smiling at a new person in class. Think about things you and your friends do. You can use your book if you get stuck for ideas. On the other side of the card, think of what you need to perform the חסד, *chesed.* For example, in the above situation all you need is to think about doing it and then do it! Try to fill as many cards as you can. When you think you've come up with every possible example, think some more! The game we'll play with the cards afterward will be more fun the more cards we have.

"Now let's have some fun with the cards we've made! Each group order your cards so the side that has an example of גמילות חסדים, *g'milut chasadim,* is facing down. Now exchange your set of cards with another group, so everyone has a new set of cards. Sit or stand in your group of four with one person holding all the cards. (Remember, the example of גמילות חסדים, *g'milut chasadim,* is facing down so you can't see it.) The first person holding the card looks at the things you do to perform this חסד, *chesed,* and pantomimes or draws examples from the card for the rest of the group. The other three people try to guess what the חסד, *chesed,* is. Keep going around the group, with everyone having a turn until you go through all the cards. If you go through all the cards before the time is up, can you think of any other games you could play with these cards?"

DICTIONARY DEFINITIONS

friend: (1) a person attached to another by feelings of affection or personal regard (2) a person who gives assistance; a patron or supporter (3) one who is on good terms with another

lovingkindness: kindness motivated by affectionate regard

neighbors: (1) a person who lives near another (2) a person who shows kindliness or helpfulness toward his/her fellows

HEBREW WORDS AND THEIR ROOTS

חבר/חברה—friend or partner

ידידות—friendship

אהוב—beloved

רעה—friend, companion

שכן—neighbor

שכנה—feminine name for God (the "Presence")

משכן—name given to the Tabernacle (a movable synagogue used by the Israelites when they wandered in the desert; within the משכן God was a "neighbor")

גומל—a benefactor

גמילות—reward

גמל—a camel (the root for this word and the two above are the same. A camel was a "rewarding animal" because in ancient times it could be used for food, clothing and, of course, transportation!)

CHALLENGING QUESTIONS THE TEACHER MAY WANT TO RAISE; OR THE GIRLS MAY RAISE

Boundaries and Friendship

Is there ever a time you should stop being a friend? How many friends should you have? Is friendship ever exclusionary, making people feel left out or rejected? Should it be? Can you ever get too close to a friend? What should we do if a friend tries to get us to do something that's not right? Is it right to try to become the friend of someone else's friend? Should friends have secrets? What do you do if your parents don't like one of your friends?

"Degrees" of Friendship

What is the relationship between friendship and popularity? Can you have a special kind of friend like a pen pal or a girl you tutor? Are these the same as your other friends? Should friends be your own age? Can they be younger? Older? By how much? Does the friendship change if the friends aren't your own age? What do you think about friendship groups? Are they more fun than one-on-one friendships? Can a boy be a friend of a girl?

Inquisitive Inquiries

What can friends teach each other? Befriending the friendless—do you want to do that? Why or why not? Do friends give each other gifts? Other than material items, what could be a gift? Does friendship need personal contact? How often? Can a friendship be sustained via instant messaging? Phone calls? Yearly visits? The Girl Scouts have a motto: "Make new friends but keep the old. One is silver, the other is gold." What do you think this means? Do you agree?

THINGS TO THINK ABOUT

We've spent time thinking about friendship and גמילות חסדים, g'milut chasadim, today. But this is just the beginning of thinking about such an important idea. A person can always become a better friend. Spend some time over the next week thinking about the list we posted and the game we played. Look at some of the examples in the book of "Random Acts of Chesed." (*The JGirl's Guide*, pp. 8–9). What acts of גמילות חסדים, g'milut chasadim, can you perform in the coming week?

OTHER SOURCES

Books/Magazines

Brashares, Ann. *The Sisterhood of the Traveling Pants*. New York: Delacorte Press, 2003. Story of four friends and the single pair of pants they share!

Burnett, Frances Hodgson. *The Secret Garden.* New York: HarperTrophy, 1998. An oldie, but goodie! An orphaned girl makes friends in her new home, with a garden being the foundation for the friendship.

Creech, Sharon. *Heartbeat.* New York: HarperCollins, 2004. Story about a girl who faces many changes: her mother's pregnancy, her grandfather's forgetfulness, and the moodiness of her best friend.

Danziger, Paula, and Ann M. Martin. *P.S. Longer Letter Later.* New York: Scholastic, 1999. Two twelve-year-old best friends continue their friendship through letter-writing after one of them moves to another state.

Isaacs, Ron. *Friendship* (instant lesson). Los Angeles: Torah Aura Productions, 2003. This instant lesson can be a springboard for the teacher's own creative lesson or be used as is.

Levoy, Myron. *Alan and Naomi.* New York: HarperCollins, 1987. The story of a friendship between two twelve-year-olds set in New York City in 1944.

Lowry, Lois. *Number the Stars.* New York: Dell, 1990. Story of two best friends, one Jewish, one not, in Copenhagen in 1943.

Montgomery, L.M. *Anne of Green Gables.* New York: Bantam Doubleday Dell, 1981. A girl on Prince Edward Island and the friends she makes. I also highly recommend the movie adaptation, *Anne of Green Gables,* directed by Kevin Sullivan. Burbank, CA: Walt Disney Home Video, 2005.

New Moon: The Magazine for Girls and Their Dreams, July/August 2002 issue has section on pen pals. This magazine is a nice general resource as well—see www.newmoon.org for subscription info.

Orgel, Doris. *The Devil in Vienna.* New York: Penguin Putnam, 2004. Story of two friends, one Jewish, the other the daughter of a Nazi SS officer.

Music

"Kol Yisrael Chaverim" by Yehuda from album Yehuda & Friends (Jerusalem Star, Inc.). The phrase *Ve'ahavta l'reyakha kamokha* appears in the song.

"Heinei Ma Tov" by Beth Schafer from album *Lev B' Lev* (Beth Schafer, 1998).

Websites

www.studio2B.org—this website is supported by the Girl Scouts of America. It focuses on six areas: Life (experiences), Style, Pulse (what's happening in the world?), Lounge (what do you want to become?), Escape (virtual trips), and Next (goals). The website should first be examined by the teacher and selections made for the girls to look at as some material is too mature for bat mitzvah–age girls.

BEING A DAUGHTER

MITZVAH

כבוד אב ואם *Kibud av va'em* (honoring father and mother)

GOALS

To build communication skills for dealing respectfully with one's parents.

To explore the difference between being a daughter as a biological or adoptive fact and being a daughter in the emotional sense.

TEXTS/QUOTES

"God accounts honor shown to parents as though it were shown to God, and, conversely, the neglect of honoring parents is regarded as an insult to God" (*Mechilta* on Exodus 20:12).

"The Hebrew midwives (Exodus 1:15) [were] Yocheved and Miriam. Miriam, who was only five years old then, went with Yocheved to assist her. She was quick [to honor her mother and to serve God (*Eitz Yosef*)]…" (*Encyclopedia of Biblical Personalities* [Mesorah, 1994], p. 337). (We have very few stories in Tanach—the Hebrew Bible—that deal with mother-daughter relationships. Discuss with the girls why this might be. Ask them what they think Yocheved taught Miriam that enabled her to develop into the great woman she became.)

"Honoring a father and mother is the most difficult mitzvah" (Jerusalem Talmud, *Peah* 1:1).

PREPARATION

Prepare scenario cards (see below) to distribute to groups. Introduce the scenarios by having a discussion about independence and "cutting the umbilical cord." When the cord is cut, the baby is separated from the mother and begins to function on its own. But because the mother is also separated from the child, the mother undergoes a transition as well. This is a good opportunity to have the girls develop some empathy for what separation and independence at this stage of their lives means for their mothers. It's also a great time to remind the girls that as they look at the scenarios, they should remember that respect for their parents must always be uppermost in their minds.

An alternative way of playing this game is to have the girls write up their own scenarios. This would be preferable as it will touch the girls where they live. However, if time constraints prevent this from happening, some suggested scenarios appear below:

Scenario #1: Your new best friend has invited you to her house for dinner and to spend the night. Neither her parents nor a supervising adult will be home. You feel you're a responsible person who should be allowed to go. Your parents don't want you to sleep over without an adult present. You argue that you baby-sit all the time and that shows how responsible you are. You think they're treating you like a little girl instead of a young adult.

Scenario #2: You want to wear makeup to school. Your parents don't want you to wear makeup at any time. You argue that everyone else wears makeup and you look stupid next to them. Your parents tell you they don't care about everyone else, only you. They feel you're too young to wear makeup. You feel they're old-fashioned and don't "get it."

Scenario #3: You've just become part of a new group of friends at school. Their clothes are edgier than what you have worn in the past. They are more independent than you've been and they do some daring, but not dangerous, things after school. Your parents aren't happy that you're hanging out with them and want you to stop. You argue that you're old enough to choose your own friends and they should trust you.

Scenario #4: Your favorite music group is playing in concert. The concert is called for 7:00–10:00 p.m. Your parents have set a curfew before the concert ends. You'll have to leave the concert early if you go. You have an argument with your parents about how inflexible they are and how special this concert is. They counter-argue that it's a school night and their curfew is a reasonable one.

Scenario #5: Your parents ask you to clean up your room. You think your room looks fine the way it is. You argue you can find everything and it has its own sense of order. Your parents argue your room is part of the house and they want it to look a certain way.

Scenario #6: Your parents always give lots of time and energy to your younger sibling. Whenever you have something to discuss they always say, "We'll talk about it later." But somehow "later" never comes. You've tried to share your feelings with your parents, but they don't make time to really talk.

BODY OF LESSON

Teacher, "Our relationship with our parents is not always smooth" (teacher may wish to share a personal story of his or her teenage years) "but showing them honor is so important that the Torah lists this mitzvah in the עשרת הדברות, the Ten Commandments. Today we're going to play a game called 'RWR—Resolve with Respect.' The purpose of this game is to help us identify some potentially difficult situations we might encounter with our parents and to brainstorm ways to deal with those situations in a manner that shows our parents honor. We'll divide into groups of five. Each group will receive a scenario card. You'll have fifteen minutes to read the scenario card and then decide how as a group you will act out the scenario. You can make up additional dialogue and use props. After the fifteen minutes are up, each group will perform its scenario for the rest of the class, one group performing at a time. After each group performs, the rest of the class will be asked to identify what the issue(s) are and how to resolve the issue(s) while still showing respect to one's parents. The group will assign one person to take notes on the suggestions made. The group will then perform its scenario again with the changes in place."

The teacher may wish to state the following before the girls begin their performances: "Being respectful of our parents, or anyone in a situation when we have strong feelings, is always a challenge. A few things to keep in mind are: speak in a respectful tone; use 'I' statements like, 'I think you don't really understand how I feel' instead of, 'You never care about my feelings.' Be a careful listener. Mirror (repeat back in your own words) what the other person has said to you. Make eye contact."

DICTIONARY DEFINITIONS

Honor: (1) high public esteem; fame; glory (2) honesty and integrity in one's beliefs and actions (3) a source of credit or distinction (4) high respect, as for worth, merit or rank

Respect: esteem for or a sense of the worth or excellence of a person, a personal quality or trait, or something considered as a manifestation of a personal quality or trait

HEBREW WORDS AND THEIR ROOTS

כבוד—honor

הורים—parents

בת—daughter

אמא-אם—mother (in Hebrew and Aramaic)

אמהות—matriarchs

צדקה-צדק—charity, righteousness, justice

CHALLENGING QUESTIONS THE TEACHER MAY WANT TO RAISE; OR THE GIRLS MAY RAISE

Communication with Parents

How do you handle differences of opinion with your parents when it comes to bedtime, curfew, and participation in independent activities? How do you speak with your parents when you're angry with them and still honor them? What do you do when all your friends want to see a movie that your parents don't want you to see? How do you regain the trust of your parents if you do something that makes them question your judgment? Can your parents also be your friends? Should they? Does the answer to this question depend upon your age?

Honor and Respect

What challenges do you face in honoring your parents? Are honor and respect equivalent? If a girl is adopted, is there a difference between honoring one's birth parents and one's adoptive parents? If you have a stepparent, and both your parents are still alive, do you owe the stepparent honor? Is it different or similar to the honor you owe your natural parents? In a given moment or situation, can you love your parents, but not like them? How does one's relationship with siblings enter into the honoring of your parents? What do you do if your friends are disrespectful to your parents (either to their face or behind their backs)? How can you dress in a way that will be "in" with your friends and also respect your parents' sense of what is appropriate? Is it possible to honor your parents and not love them?

Inquisitive Inquiries

Can you be a daughter to someone who isn't in your family? As you look at the choices your parents make, which will you make differently when you're a parent? Which will you make the same?

THINGS TO THINK ABOUT

Just as participating in an activity together (such as volunteering at a soup kitchen) can help you become closer to your parents, so can learning together. Consider finding a topic you and your parents are interested in and investigating it together. Maybe you and your parents both love music, but different types of music. Think about educating each other as to your tastes. Just like you, your parents are always growing and learning. Doing it together can be great fun and bring you closer together. Think about interviewing your parents to find out what life was like when they were exactly your age. Use Shireen Dodson's *Mother-Daughter Book Club* (see below) to help you and your mom start your own book club.

OTHER SOURCES

Books/Magazines

Baskin, Nora Raleigh. *What Every Girl (Except Me) Knows*. Boston: Little, Brown, 2001. Twelve-year-old Gabby searches for her mother when things between her father and his girlfriend don't work out.

Dodson, Shireen. *Mother-Daughter Book Club: How Ten Busy Mothers and Daughters Came Together to Talk, Laugh and Learn through Their Love of Reading*. New York: HarperCollins, 1997. This book provides old and new literature for mothers and daughters to explore together. A special feature of the book is the "thought questions" given after each entry.

———. *100 Books for Girls to Grow On.* New York: HarperCollins, 1998. Wonderful resource containing descriptions of books, discussion questions, activities and field trips.

Fritz, Jean. *Homesick, My Own Story.* New York: Penguin Putnam, 1982. The author's fictionalized story of her childhood in China in the 1920s, includes photographs.

Grishaver, Joel Lurie. *Honoring Parents* (instant lesson) Los Angeles: Torah Aura Productions, 2000. This instant lesson can be a springboard for the teacher's own creative lesson or be used as is.

L'Engle, Madeleine. *Meet the Austins.* New York: Dell, 1985. Story of twelve-year-old Vicky and her adjustment to an orphan who joins her family.

Ryan, Pam Muñoz. *Becoming Naomi Leon.* New York: Scholastic, 2004. Naomi runs away to Mexico with her great-grandmother and younger brother in search of her father.

Sturtevant, Katherine. *At the Sign of the Star.* New York: Farrar, Straus and Giroux, 2002. Set in seventeenth-century London, Meg dreams of becoming a bookseller and someday inheriting her widowed father's bookstore.

Lesson 3 EATING

MITZVOT

מאכל רעבים *Ma'akhil re'eyvim* (feeding the hungry); הכנסת אורחים *Hakhnasat orchim* (inviting guests); כשרות *Kashrut* (sanctifying food)

GOALS

To recognize that Judaism sees the consumption of food as an elevated, spiritual activity.

To examine body images of women through art and recognize that there isn't one standard of health and beauty.

To understand the connection in Judaism between food and community.

TEXTS/QUOTES

כל דכפין ייתי ויכול "All who are hungry let them come and eat!" (Passover Haggadah).

כי אני ה' א–להים והתקדשתם והייתם קדושים כי קדוש אני "For I am Adonai your God. You shall sanctify yourselves and be holy, for I am holy" (Leviticus 11:44).

PREPARATION

Bring photos of paintings of women by Renoir, Matisse, Picasso, and Ingres. (Teacher should note the paintings by Ingres will most likely be nudes. If there is concern about using them, don't.) Have sticky notes, 3" x 5" cards, and pencils available for the stations (see below for more information on the stations). Create a blank food group chart, and have a filled-in food group chart. Have copies in Hebrew and English translation of the blessings before eating, ברכת המזון, Grace after Meals, and the ברכה אחרונה, short blessings after meals. Be sure to include the special additions to ברכת המזון said at a *brit milah* and a wedding. Large chart paper will also be needed.

BODY OF LESSON

Chapter 3 in *The JGirl's Guide* contains a great diversity of ideas. Feeding the hungry, inviting guests, *kashrut,* and eating disorders are all discussed. You may wish to divide this lesson into two sessions.

The girls will rotate between three stations. At the first station are photos of paintings by Renoir, Matisse, Picasso, and Ingres, and 3" x 5" cards. At the second station are sticky notes and a chart listing the food groups. At the third station are copies in Hebrew and English translation of the blessings before eating, along with a short description of what blessing goes with what food (for example, בורא פרי העץ on fruits), ברכת המזון, Grace after Meals, and the ברכה אחרונה, shorter blessings after meals.

At the first station each girl will look at the paintings, write on an index card one word that describes the body images of the women, and place the card face down near the painting. The teacher will collect the cards after the girls have visited all of the stations. There will be a whole group discussion about the words on the cards and what they say about body image.

At the second station each girl will write five of her favorite foods on separate sticky notes. She will then place each note on the blank chart in the category in which she thinks it belongs (for example, banana under "fruits and vegetables"). The teacher will post a completed food chart and the girls will compare how they grouped the foods. (To enhance the learning experience, the chart the teacher creates can have the Hebrew words for each category. See Hebrew Words and Their Roots for assistance.)

At the third station the girls will examine the various *brachot* and determine why the wording for each blessing appears as it does (for example, why is the blessing over bread, "who brings up bread from the earth"?). The girls will look closely at the ברכת המזון, Grace after Meals, and list on chart paper examples of ties between the community sharing bread and the ברכת המזון. They will be asked to draw conclusions between the *mitzvot* of מאכל רעבים, הכנסת אורחים, and כשרות.

DICTIONARY DEFINITIONS

Hospitality: the friendly reception and treatment of guests or strangers

Hunger: a compelling need or desire for food

Image: (1) a mental representation, idea, conception (2) form, appearance, semblance (3) to reflect the likeness of, mirror

HEBREW WORDS AND THEIR ROOTS

אוכל—food

ברכות—blessings

ברכת המזון—Grace after Meals (said after meals where bread is eaten)

בְּרָכָה אַחֲרוֹנָה—short blessings after meals (said in meals where no bread is eaten)

גּוּף—body

פֵּרוֹת—fruits

יְרָקוֹת—vegetables

לֶחֶם—bread

חָלָב—milk

בָּשָׂר—meat

דָּג—fish

CHALLENGING QUESTIONS THE TEACHER MAY WANT TO RAISE; OR THE GIRLS MAY RAISE

הַכְנָסַת אוֹרְחִים—Inviting Guests

In today's world strangers aren't always safe people. How do you carry on in the tradition of Abraham and Sarah, and be hospitable to strangers? What kinds of things can you do to make a guest feel comfortable in your home? If the person is your age? Older? An adult? Someone who doesn't speak English? What happens if you invite someone to your home on a number of occasions and they never invite you to their home? Do you keep inviting them?

כַּשְׁרוּת—*Kashrut*

If you want to explore keeping kosher and your family doesn't, how could you do that in a manner respectful to your family and your self-exploration? If your family doesn't keep a kosher home and you want to invite a friend who does keep kosher to your house for a meal, how would you go about doing that? What do you do when you're invited to someone's home whose level of *kashrut* is different from yours? How can not eating milk right after meat, or not eating certain foods, help us become conscious of what we put in our bodies and help to refine our relationship with the world around us?

מַאֲכָל רְעֵבִים—Feeding the Hungry

Is this mitzvah limited to people who are homeless? If you feed a younger sibling are you fulfilling this mitzvah? How about if you cook dinner for your family? How are we like God when we fulfill this mitzvah? Is there a difference between working in a soup kitchen, feeding the people there, and serving food at your home table?

Inquisitive Inquiries

How do you view food? Is it a gift? A temptation? A way to celebrate? How can you eat more healthily or exercise if your family doesn't? What is appropriate exercise for a girl your age? Do you think there's a difference between what boys consume in a meal and what girls consume in a meal? Quality? Quantity? There seems to be a mixed message in the media about food and eating. There are advertisements for healthy eating and exercise, while there are also photographs of super-thin models in all the magazines. What do you think a healthy body looks like? What should you do if you see someone in the girl's bathroom purging after a meal? When does watching what you're eating for balance in your meals cross over to obsessing about food? Rabbi Jennifer Rebecca Marx is quoted in *The JGirl's Guide* as saying, "An eating disorder is not about food: it is about being empty on the inside. It is feeling that you have no right to exist. If you are anorexic, you are trying to make yourself disappear; if you are bulimic or a compulsive overeater, you are trying to fill the emptiness." Discuss this quote. What is Rabbi Marx saying about the relationship between food and a person's self-image?

THINGS TO THINK ABOUT

In Judaism, even something as simple as eating is seen as a spiritual activity. In the coming weeks, give some consideration to the types of food you're eating and how you're eating. Enjoy eating and appreciate the opportunities to share meals with friends and family. Sharing meals with other people brings spirituality to eating, too.

OTHER SOURCES

Books/Magazines

"The Fight of Her Life," *Girl's Life Magazine,* December/January 2005, Vol. 11, Issue 3 (pp. 62–63, 79). Story of Caroline Rowley, fifteen, who has diabetes.

Kolodny, Nancy J. *When Food's a Foe: How You Can Confront and Conquer Your Eating Disorder.* Boston: Little, Brown, 1987. Hands-on book with checklists, questionnaires, and exercises.

Petersen, P.J. *I Hate Company.* New York: Viking Penguin, 1998. Dan resents his loss of privacy when his mother offers to temporarily share their apartment with an old friend and her three-year-old.

Ward, Brian R. *Diet and Nutrition.* London: Watts Franklin, 1987. Contains nutritional values in short sections with simple wording and photos.

Lesson 4 RESTING

MITZVAH

שמירת שבת *Shmirat Shabbat* (observance of a day of rest)

GOALS

To examine the definitions of work and rest and apply them to Shabbat.

To begin to understand the relationship between Shabbat and the Jewish people.

To explore the depth of "אשת חיל," *"Eishet Chayil,"* and develop a personal connection with the song.

To use the "אשת חיל," *"Eishet Chayil,"* project as a means of creating a closer tie with female role models in the girls' lives.

TEXTS/QUOTES

כל כבודה בת מלך פנימה "The true majesty of a royal daughter is inside her" (Psalm 45).

PREPARATION

Copies for all the girls of "אשת חיל," *"Eishet Chayil,"* in Hebrew and English. Gather drawing paper, colored pencils, watercolor paper, watercolors, tissue paper, glue, scissors, and clay for group use.

BODY OF LESSON

Teacher: "Today we're going to be looking closely at the special song from Proverbs 'אשת חיל,' *'Eishet Chayil,'* which is sung on Friday night in many Jewish homes, usually by a husband to his wife. This song praises women. We're going to begin by pairing up to read 'אשת חיל,' *'Eishet Chayil.'* Read one line in Hebrew" (if girls aren't able to do this, just use the English) "and then the same line in English translation. With your partner find one verse that speaks to you." (Each girl can choose a different verse.) "It could remind you of something you aspire to achieve; it could reflect a quality you recognize in a special woman in your life whom you admire; it could be that you just like the poetry of the line! Whatever the reason, once you have the verse, you and your partner rewrite it in your own words. Then choose an art medium with which you wish to work. You don't have to be an artist to do this project. Your completed art work can be abstract or literal. The only requirements you have are that each of you must make your own project; you are all encouraged to get ideas and assistance from the other girls in the class; each project should somehow incorporate the original chosen verse as well as the verse in your own words.

"Here are some things to think about while creating your project: Use of color—how can the colors help establish mood, attitude? Use of shape—are your shapes going to be smooth or angled? Use of texture—how will the materials you use affect your piece?"

When the pieces are completed suggest to the girls that they may wish to present this art work to a special woman in their lives with an explanation of the project.

DICTIONARY DEFINITIONS

Rest: (1) the refreshing quiet or repose of sleep (2) refreshing ease or inactivity after exertion or labor (3) relief or freedom, especially from anything that wearies, troubles, or disturbs

Work: (1) exertion or effort directed to produce or accomplish something, labor, toil (2) productive or operative activity (3) employment

Valor: boldness or determination in facing great danger, heroic courage, bravery

HEBREW WORDS AND THEIR ROOTS

הדור מצוה—beautification/embellishment of a mitzvah

אשת חיל—woman of valor

נרות של שבת—Shabbat candles

זמירות—Shabbat songs

עבודה—work, labor

מלאכה—work that exercises control over ones environment

בריאת העולם—creation of the world

בית המקדש—Temple (literally, House of Sanctity)

חבורה—group of friends

סדור—prayerbook

תפילה—prayer

קבלת שבת—receiving the Shabbat (Friday night service)

סעודה שלישית—third meal on Shabbat

הבדלה—separation ceremony between Shabbat and the new week

נשמה יתרה—extra soul

CHALLENGING QUESTIONS THE TEACHER MAY WANT TO RAISE; OR THE GIRLS MAY RAISE:

Theological Questions

Talking and thinking about God may not be something we usually do. Shabbat is a great time to think about God and ask theological questions (that is, questions about God). How did God decide to create the world? What is God's relationship with us? What's our relationship with God? What does it mean to have an "extra" soul—נשמה יתרה—on Shabbat? What does the quote by Ahad Ha'am on p. 53 of the *The JGirl's Guide,* "More than the Jewish people have kept Shabbat, Shabbat has kept the Jewish people," mean? What do you think he meant by *Shabbat?* Does Shabbat still "keep" the Jewish people?

Shabbat Questions

Why are we told to "keep" and "remember" the Shabbat? If we "keep" the Shabbat aren't we automatically "remembering" it? Why are the concepts of both *Shabbat haMalkah* (representing structure and order) and *Shabbat haKallah* (representing emotion and passion) important to the idea of Shabbat? Do you think Shabbat can exist with only one of these concepts? Why do we still set aside a piece of dough when we bake challah? Do you think this is an important mitzvah to perform today? How do you define work? Look at the list of 39 *Avot Melacha* of Shabbat (prohibitions of Shabbat—see **Other Resources** at the end of this lesson). How do you understand them in modern terms? How do you understand the idea of welcoming the Shabbat Bride? How can you personalize your Shabbat experience? The *Havdalah* service is multisensory, incorporating sounds, sight, smell. Why do you think it was structured that way? How does this help us leave Shabbat and enter the new week?

Inquisitive Inquiries

The concept of *na'aseh venishma* (we will do and we will hear) is not an easy one. What do you think of this order of doing before understanding? Do you always understand things before you do them? Should you? What do you do if you'd like to go to services but can't find a synagogue close by that you enjoy attending?

THINGS TO THINK ABOUT

Shabbat is a great time to catch up with friends and family, think deeply, sing songs, and just be! Sometimes there's a book or an article you've wanted to read, but you've been too busy with homework or the numerous activities of the week. Shabbat's a good time to do that reading. There are some suggestions of Jewish books under the **Other Sources** section.

OTHER SOURCES

Books/Magazines

Read your local Jewish newspaper or magazine to be current with things happening in your community.

Chait, Rabbi Baruch. *The 39 Avoth Melacha of Shabbat.* Jerusalem: Feldheim, 1993. A fun, illustrated look at the prohibitions of Shabbat.

Gellman, Marc. *God's Mailbox.* New York: William Morrow, 1998. Humorous stories about the Bible.

Kolatch, Alfred J. *The Jewish Book of Why.* New York: Penguin, 2003. See the chapter on Shabbat.

Schram, Peninnah. *Jewish Stories One Generation Tells Another.* Northvale, NJ: Jason Aronson, 1993. A variety of Jewish stories culled from traditional and folk tales.

Schwartz, Howard, and Barbara Rush. *A Coat for the Moon and Other Jewish Tales.* Philadelphia: Jewish Publication Society, 2000. A collection of stories.

———. *The Diamond Tree: Jewish Tales from around the World.* New York: HarperTrophy, 1998. A collection of stories.

Segal, Sheila. *Women of Valor: Stories of Great Jewish Women Who Helped Shape the 20th Century.* Springfield, NJ: Behrman House, 1996. Stories and photographs of modern Jewish women. Many of these women are still alive. This could lead to a project involving the girls doing research and possibly contacting these individuals.

Segal, Yocheved. *Our Sages Showed the Way.* Jerusalem: Feldheim, 1982. A collection of *midrashim* and *aggadot* written in story form. This is part of a series.

Women of Reform Judaism. *The Gift of Prayer: The Spirituality of Jewish Women.* New York: URJ Press, 2002. Beautiful art work and moving poetry.

Music

Bat-ella. *Rhythm of the Land: New Renditions of Israeli Favorites.* Israel: Bat-ella Berman, 1997.

Friedman, Debbie. *And You Shall Be a Blessing.* San Diego: Sounds Write, 1997.

———. *Renewal of Spirit.* San Diego: Sounds Write, 1997.

———. *The World of Your Dreams.* San Diego: Sounds Write, 2002.

Hirschhorn, Linda, with Vocolot. *Gather Round.* Berkeley, CA: Kehila Publications: 1989.

Kol Achai. *Bni.* NY: M & M Enterprises.

Simon, Jon. *New Traditions 2.* Bethesda, MD: Silver Lining Records, 1990.

Veroba, Gershon. *Then and Now.* S.M.T. Productions, 1993.

Movies

Kay, Michelle. *Ha-motzi Lechem min Ha-aretz.* (Waltham, Mass.: The Hadassah-Brandeis Institute, 2002). Documentary film, fifteen minutes.

Lesson 5
FEELING GOOD ABOUT MY BODY

MITZVOT

שתפי למעשה בראשית *Shutafey l'ma'aseh bereishit* (partners in creation); בצלם א–להים *Betzelem Elohim* (in the image of God)

GOALS

To feel a sense of awe about the world and therefore about ourselves.

To recognize that being created in the image of God means that we are in partnership with God to keep the world going.

TEXTS/QUOTES

ברא אתו זכר ונקבה ברא אתם בצלמו בצלם א–להים "Thus God created human beings in God's own image; in the image of God, God created them; male and female God created them" (Genesis 1:27).

"One view of being created in the image of God is that the qualities of God are in each of us" (*The JGirl's Guide,* p. 75).

"We are in partnership with God regarding all creation—animals and plants, oceans and rivers, mountains and plains. A partnership is a cooperative effort. In this case, we are in a cooperative effort with God to keep creation going" (*The JGirl's Guide,* p. 73).

PREPARATION

Each triad of girls should have a camera. (Digital cameras are preferable, as you can use them with a computer; otherwise, regular or disposable cameras are fine. If cameras are not available, the girls could draw from nature, look at photographs of nature, or look at magazines that feature nature. The point is to have visual representations of nature.) This lesson is meant to take place over several sessions and involves a field trip. If your school is situated on grounds with trees, animals, and birds, you can do this lesson on school property. If not, take your students to a nearby park or nature walk. Each girl should have a pad of paper and pencil.

Chapter 5, "Feeling Good about My Body," Chapter 6, "Liking Myself," and Chapter 10, "Becoming Myself," explore similar, complimentary ideas. You may wish to consider this when planning your lessons and selecting the order in which you present your lessons.

BODY OF LESSON

Lesson 7 focuses on girls' bodies. By contrast, Lesson 5 spotlights the role we play as partners with God to keep the world going and emphasizes our relationship with nature. The teacher can choose to lead a whole group discussion, divide the girls into small groups, or have girls in *chevruta* (see Introduction). Because these questions are so challenging, the *chevruta* may be the best option for this lesson.

The teacher can pose these questions or they can be on the board, or on a sheet for group discussion: "What do you think this quote from *The JGirl's Guide* means in practical terms? 'We are in partnership with God regarding all creation—animals and plants, oceans and rivers, mountains and plains. A partnership is a cooperative effort. In this case, we are in a cooperative effort with God to keep creation going' (*The JGirl's Guide*, p. 73).

"As partners with God we're charged not only with caring for the world, but also with appreciating its beauty. When God evaluates the creation of the world, the words 'כִּי טוֹב'—'it was good'—are used. Each day God creates something different and the creation of the world is a process. God doesn't make everything simultaneously in a single moment (although it could have been done that way.)" At this point the teacher may wish to review with the girls the Creation story in Chapter One of Genesis. "Why do you think God created the world in stages? What's the significance of the types of things that are created each day? Some things are created by separating pieces out from a larger whole, like separation of the waters; do we ever 'create' in this way? Give some examples. Why does God evaluate God's work? Can't we assume God's creation will be good? Why does God give the blessing to be fruitful and multiply to the animals and people? What other meanings could the words 'פְּרוּ וּרְבוּ'—'be fruitful and multiply'—have other than reproduction in a physical sense?

"Connecting with the world of which we are a part is a way to feel good about ourselves. Have you ever noticed that taking a walk outside in nature can relax your body and spirit? Sometimes just sitting outside in the yard has a calming effect. Doctors and dentists understand this too. Next time you're in one of their offices notice what kinds of photos or prints they have on the walls and ceilings. Often the photos or prints are of scenes from nature. Our bodies are containers for our souls and so it's also important to take care of our souls. Taking a really good look at the world around us is a way to sensitize our souls and develop our spirituality.

"We're going to spend today's session (and maybe a second session) on a field trip. You'll be working in groups of three, with several tasks. Task number one is to be observers of the world around you and see how various elements are connected. As an example, take the time to study a tree very closely. How many creatures do you see inhabiting the tree? (Insects count too!) How is the tree connected to its surroundings? Task number two is to write down any observations you have. Be very free-style about this. You can write single words, feelings, poetic phrases; whatever you feel moved to write. Task number three is for each girl to have a chance to photograph (or draw). Take the time to look around you and frame your photos. You may want to zoom in very close (the bark of a tree up close looks very different from what it looks like from afar) or blur your photo. Set up your photo and have the other two girls look through the lens and share what they see. There isn't a limit or requirement for the number of photographs you take. Just take time to appreciate the beauty of the world."

Next session: The photos should be downloaded into the computer and printed out, or developed. Poster board should be available for the final steps of the project. (If a digital camera was used the girls could use a computer program for their final product rather than poster board.) The teacher should post the following quotes for the girls to see:

בצלמו בצלם א-להים ברא אתו זכר ונקבה ברא אתם "Thus God created human beings in God's own image; in the image of God, God created them; male and female God created them" (Genesis 1:27).

"One view of being created in the image of God is that the qualities of God are in each of us" (*The JGirl's Guide*, p. 75).

"We are in partnership with God regarding all creation—animals and plants, oceans and rivers, mountains and plains. A partnership is a cooperative effort. In this case, we are in a cooperative effort with God to keep creation going" (*The JGirl's Guide*, p. 73).

Teacher: "Look at your photographs and your written observations. Create a montage from your materials. Your goal is to try to re-create the sense of wonderment you felt when photographing/viewing these items for the person looking at your montage. You are encouraged to use one or more of the quotes or a segment of the quote in your montage."

DICTIONARY DEFINITIONS

Creation: (1) act of producing or causing to exist (2) the original bringing into existence of the universe by God (3) an original product of the mind, especially an imaginative artistic work

Exercise: (1) bodily or mental exercise, especially for the sake of training or improvement (2) putting into action, use, operation, or effect (the exercise of willpower)

Leisure: (1) freedom from the demands of work or duty (2) free or unoccupied time (3) unhurried ease (4) without haste; slowly

Partner: (1) one who shares or is associated with another in some action or endeavor (2) player on the same side, or team, as another

HEBREW WORDS AND THEIR ROOTS

רוחניות—spirituality

בצלם א-להים —in God's image

שֻׁתָּפוּת–שֻׁתָּף—partner, partnership

עֵצִים–עֵץ—tree, trees

צִפֳּרִים–צִפּוֹר—bird, birds

הַר—mountain

נַחַל—river

יָם—ocean

CHALLENGING QUESTIONS THE TEACHER MAY WANT TO RAISE; OR THE GIRLS MAY RAISE

Body and Soul Questions

What's the connection between your body and soul? If your body is feeling out-of-sorts, how is your soul affected, and vice versa? Can perceiving beauty in the world have an effect on your body? How can you honor your body on a daily basis? Why is leisure time so important? Is there a difference between spending leisure time watching a video or going for a walk outside? Do you prefer one over the other? Have you learned to listen to your body? Do you know when it's tired, hungry? How do you balance the needs of maintaining a healthy body with your need for independence? (When everyone else is eating junk food, or staying up really late, what do you do when your body tells you that those things are unhealthy, but you want to fit in?)

Theological Questions

The other parts of the world are not created in God's image. Why do you think God created us in God's image? What does the statement "God is said to be the third partner, with the parents, in the conception of a child" (*The JGirls Guide*, p. 75) mean to you? Have you thought about how God wants you to use the special gifts of your unique talents and personality?

Inquisitive Inquiries

What does it mean to be a partner with God as a twelve- or thirteen-year-old? *Sanhedrin* 4:37 says, "To save one person is to save an entire world." How can saving one person save the entire world? Improving your physical health is often easier to tackle than improving your emotional and spiritual health. Where could you go for guidance on the latter two? How do you respond if a friend begins to smoke or do drugs? What if your friend wants you to smoke or do drugs? How can the idea of being created בְּצֶלֶם אֱ-לֹהִים, in God's image, help you in these situations?

THINGS TO THINK ABOUT

Our bodies are an awesome gift from God and our souls are, too. It's important to nourish both on a regular basis. What nourished us as children isn't the same as what will nourish us as adults. Judaism sees our bodies as being holy. We're encouraged to take care of our mind, body, and spirit. Enjoy this time of exploration! Reread the "Do It" section in *The JGirl's Guide* on pp. 78–79. Try to add at least two items under each category of "Body," "Mind," and "Soul."

OTHER SOURCES

Books/Magazines

Cohen, Sasha, with Amanda Maciel. *Fire on Ice: Autobiography of a Champion Figure Skater.* New York: HarperCollins, 2005. Autobiography of the Jewish athlete.

Cordes, Helen. *Girl Power in the Mirror: A Book about Girls, Their Bodies, and Themselves.* Minneapolis: Lerner Publications, 2000. Suggests ways for girls to develop self-esteem and become assertive in the face of pressures from advertisers, family, and peers to have a "perfect" body.

Jukes, Marvis and Lilian Cheung. *Be Healthy! It's a Girl Thing: Food, Fitness, and Feeling Great.* New York: Random House, 2003. A guide for adolescent girls on how to stay healthy and fit, with information on nutrition and exercise.

Luby, Thia. *Yoga for Teens: How to Improve Your Fitness, Confidence, Appearance, and Health—and Have Fun Doing It!* Santa Fe: Clear Light, 1999. Explains the philosophy and benefits of yoga to teenagers, and provides photographs and step-by-step instructions for a variety of poses.

Schuerger, Michele and Tina Schwager. *The Right Moves: A Girl's Guide to Getting Fit and Feeling Good.* Minneapolis: Free Spirit, 1998. Explains how girls can achieve total fitness by focusing on three broad areas: developing a positive self-image, choosing nutritious foods, and exercising regularly.

Music

One way to nourish your soul is to listen to music. If you've never listened to classical music before, consider closing your eyes and listening to the music of Chopin, Liszt, or Mendelssohn.

Other

"Jewish + Female = Athlete" a calendar and exhibit by The Hadassah-Brandeis Institute. Visit www.brandeis.edu/hbi or call 781-736-2064 for information.

Lesson 6
LIKING MYSELF

MITZVAH

צניעות *Tzniut* (dignity through modesty)

GOALS

To discover the Jewish connection between light and soul.

To explore what it means to be a light in God's lamp.

To become more comfortable seeing the beauty in one's self.

TEXTS/QUOTES

נר ה' נשמת אדם "The lamp of God is the soul of a person" (Proverbs 20:27).

"The mitzvah of *tzniut* is about 'modesty'—in the sexual sense (how we dress and how we carry ourselves) as well as in the sense of humility (not being arrogant and vain, and understanding the importance of respecting others). It is based on self-esteem" (*The JGirl's Guide,* p. 86).

"Rabbi Yochanan said, 'Had the Torah not been given we would have learned modesty from a cat, not to commit theft from an ant, not to commit adultery from a dove, the proper manner of conduct for marital relations from a rooster who first appeases its mate and then has relations with it" (Tractate *Eruvin* 100b; translation from *Tractate Eruvin,* Schottenstein Edition, New York: Mesorah Publications, 1998).

PREPARATION

It will be important to establish a certain mood in the room for this lesson. You may wish to prepare the girls by setting an expectation for the sound level for this exercise.

BODY OF LESSON

Teacher: "Light is a very important image in Judaism. I've written two words on the board: נר, lamp or candle, and נשמה, soul. I'm going to turn off all the lights and light a single candle. In groups of four, take a few minutes to observe the candle. Think about how a נר (lamp or candle) affects its surroundings. For example, it gives off light. Talk very quietly in your groups about your observations. Then list all the things you've observed. When you think you've listed everything, think again!" (Possible responses: heat, beauty, seems transparent and hard to touch but has a physical presence, rainbow colors, reflection, soft, harsh.) "Light and candles are often compared to the soul. You'll notice that's the second word I've written on the board. Go back to your groups and discuss and write down all the ways you think a person's soul can be compared to a light.

"There is a beautiful quote from Proverbs: נר ה' נשמת אדם, the lamp of God is the soul of a person. What does this verse mean to you in light of your recent observations?" (The teacher should at this point write the whole quote on the board or have it on a card to post.)

"Chapter 6 in *The JGirl's Guide,* 'Liking Myself,' talks about צניעות (dignity through modesty). One way to look at the verse נר ה' נשמת אדם is to say that we are a reflection of God's light. That's a pretty powerful idea! A single light, unlike a blazing fire, isn't ostentatious; in a way, it's actually modest. On the other hand, its presence is definitely felt and noticed. It is unique. Notice that the flame is never quite the same from moment to moment, just as each of us is unique and never quite the same from moment to moment. Because each of us is in the world, we light the lamp of God. It's important to reflect upon our unique beauty and celebrate it! Everyone knows someone who literally lights up the room. Maybe it's the way they greet you, or smile. They could be very quiet or energetic. Think about this person. Write them a letter. (You don't have to actually send it to them, though you can if you want. This is to help you think about yourself.) In the letter share the special qualities you see in them. When we notice these things about others it helps us to refine our character as well. Think about your language as you write the letter. How can the words you use be modest in nature? How can they reflect the light in God's lamp?"

If you'd like to assign homework to the girls, you might reproduce the quote from *Eruvin* (see p. 32) on a sheet of paper. Ask them to reflect on the use of the cat in this passage to portray the character of modesty. Do they agree or disagree with the choice of the cat? If they disagree, what other animal would they choose? Encourage them to share the passage with their parents and discuss it with them.

Another fun homework assignment would be to have the girls look through teen magazines and cut out two pictures, one representing modest dress and one immodest dress. Ask the girls to paste the photos into their יומן and write about the photo they prefer and why. The next session the girls can share their photos and entries. They could also explain and debate how and why they categorized the photos.

DICTIONARY DEFINITIONS

Confidence: (1) full trust (2) certitude; assurance

Humility: modest sense of one's own importance

Integrity: (1) soundness of and adherence to moral principle and character; uprightness; honesty (2) the state of being whole, entire

Modesty: (1) freedom from vanity, boastfulness (2) regard for decency of behavior, speech, dress (3) simplicity; moderation

Self-esteem: an objective respect for or favorable impression of oneself

HEBREW WORDS AND THEIR ROOTS

צניעות—modesty

ענוה—modesty, humility

נשמה—soul

ביטחון עצמי—confidence (literally having faith in one's self)

יופי—beauty

CHALLENGING QUESTIONS THE TEACHER MAY WANT TO RAISE; OR THE GIRLS MAY RAISE

Inquisitive Inquiries

Modesty extends beyond how one dresses. How can modesty be reflected in the way you furnish your house? In the way a table is set for a meal? In the items served at the meal? How one speaks to others, in both tone and actual language? Is *tzniut* an absolute value (the same for everyone)? How would you rate the modesty level of language on television? In your school? Among your friends? How you speak? What's the difference between being beautiful and helping others feel beautiful? Is self-esteem something you're born with or do you have to develop it? Are there other factors besides body image that contribute to self-esteem? Is being graceful a part of modesty? Is modesty achievable by anyone at any age?

THINGS TO THINK ABOUT

Liking yourself isn't always an easy task, particularly when you're going through so many changes! But each of us is an individual possessing great beauty. In the next few weeks take time to pay attention to the people around you. Notice when someone speaks in a modest manner, when someone is dressed modestly, or moves in a way that is modest. Can you define what you see to someone else? How can you emulate what you see?

OTHER SOURCES

Books/Magazines

DeBear, Kirsten. *Be Quiet, Marina!* New York: Star Bright Books, 2001. A noisy little girl with cerebral palsy and a quiet little girl with Down's syndrome learn to play together and eventually become best friends.

Manolson, Gila. *Outside, Inside: A Fresh Look at Tzniut.* New York: Targum/Feldheim, 1997. This book isn't specifically written for the teen, but it may be valuable to the teacher. Certain passages may be helpful to share with the girls.

Metzger, Lois. *Barry's Sister.* New York: Simon & Schuster, 1992. Twelve-year-old Ellen's loathing for her new baby brother, Barry, who has cerebral palsy, gradually changes to a fierce, obsessive love, and she must find a proper balance for her life.

Olitzky, Kerry M., and Joel Lurie Grishaver. *Modesty: Body Ethics* (instant lesson). Los Angeles: Torah Aura Productions, 2001. An excellent resource with many thought provoking questions.

Lesson 7 BECOMING A WOMAN

MITZVOT

קְדוֹשִׁים תִּהְיוּ *K'doshim tihyu* (you shall be holy); כָּל כְּבוּדָה בַת מֶלֶךְ פְּנִימָה *Kol k'vodah bat melekh p'nimah* (the true majesty of a royal daughter is inside her)

GOALS

To focus the girls' attention on the idea of separation/holiness.

TEXTS/QUOTES

"Holiness is an inner quality that each person has, a quality that allows us to connect with something greater than us and greater than our lives here on earth…. *K'doshim tihyu* means that you inhabit a sacred space and your body is a sacred space, a holy temple" (*The JGirl's Guide,* p. 101).

PREPARATION

Find out if there is a *mikvah* near you. If there is, make plans to visit it. If there are several, find out what the differences are among them and choose one that will be best for the girls. Or you may wish to visit all of them. Make certain you visit the *mikvah* before bringing the whole group. Be certain you have a knowledgeable person giving the tour. In some communities there are women who run classes explaining the rules of the *mikvah*. See if you can contact one of these women to come to class before your visit to answer any questions the girls might have. *Mikvah* is a transformational ritual. Explain to the girls that *mikva'ot* are used for many purposes, including conversion, by some men before Shabbat and holidays, and by men and women before their wedding. You may wish to research information about a new *mikvah* that recently opened in Newton, Massachusetts, called Mayyim Hayyim. The contact information is: Mayyim Hayyim Living Waters Community Mikveh and Education Center, 1838 Washington Street, Newton, MA 02466, 617-244-1836.

If you are unable to visit a *mikvah* you may be able to have a woman who regularly uses the *mikvah* join your group to speak about her experiences. Since *mikva'ot* are also used by those who have converted and women who have recently given birth, these are also people you may wish to invite to speak to the girls.

The teacher should be aware that this lesson can be successful only if an atmosphere of trust and intimacy has been achieved in the group. Menstruation, *mikvah*, and קדושה are not light topics! You may wish to have the girls prepare for this lesson by taking a few minutes to write down their thoughts about these topics in their יומן. (The יומן allows girls who are shy or uncomfortable sharing their feelings to express themselves in a safe environment. Tell the girls to put their יומן in a very safe place as it is private.) The teacher should be prepared to share her or his thoughts, but allow the girls to take the lead.

BODY OF LESSON

Teacher: "Chapter 7 in *The JGirl's Guide* is about 'Becoming a Woman.' One of the topics of discussion in this chapter is קדושה, holiness or separateness. As Jews, we focus on holiness in many different ways. We separate the days of the week from Shabbat. We make Shabbat a holy/separate day. The *Havdalah* service specifically refers to this idea." (See Chapter 4, "Resting," in *The JGirl's Guide*.) "The laws of *kashrut* help us separate those foods we eat from those we don't." (See Chapter 3, "Eating," in *The JGirl's Guide*.)

"Judaism sees our bodies as being holy and that means treating them with dignity and respect. In Judaism bodies are considered to be קדוש, holy/separate, because, as the Torah says, we are made בצלם א-להים, in the image of God. This means all people, including those with major disabilities—either physical or mental.

"Menstruation is a biological process indicating your body's maturation. Little girls do not menstruate from the time they are born, but only begin to do so in their teens. Why? The onset of menstruation—also called menses—varies enormously among girls and generations. In the concentration camps, many women stopped menstruating. Why do you think that happened?

"Menstruation is also a miracle. We never know exactly when the first period will come. People have different attitudes toward it. Some are very negative. What is your attitude? If you have a negative attitude, one way to turn it around and make it positive is to realize that when you begin menstruating, you become a member of the world of women. 'Menstruation is a miracle that signals your capacity to bring life into being. Traditional Judaism uses menstruation as a reason for a woman to have time for herself, to be with her body alone' (*The JGirl's Guide*, p. 105). We're going to spend some time exploring what this quote means.

"You've read a bit about the *mikvah*. We're going to learn more about the *mikvah* by taking a field trip to visit one." (If you can arrange for someone to come speak to the girls in advance, this would be a good place for that to happen.) At this point the teacher should have the girls split off into small groups to discuss why water is used as the substance through which we sanctify our bodies. The teacher may wish to provide some leading questions, such as: (1) What is unique about the properties of water? (Possible answers—it's clear; refreshing; a large percentage of our bodies are water; it's natural; it makes you feel clean; it combines the elements of oxygen and hydrogen; two gases that together form a liquid.) (2) Why do we use a percentage of rain water? (Possible answers—reconnecting with the earth and nature; freshness; "living" water to affirm the life giving force a woman possesses.)

After returning from visiting the *mikvah:* "We've already spoken about the importance of proper nutrition and rest for our bodies. During the time a woman is menstruating she has an opportunity to focus on herself, to have time for herself and space to herself. It's a time for rejuvenation.

"After immersing in the *mikvah* some women have the custom of reciting a short prayer that begins with the words יהי רצון—may it be your will. A translation of the beginning of this prayer is, 'May it be Your will, Lord our God and the God of our forefathers, that the Temple be rebuilt, speedily in our days.…' Women who say this prayer do so with the hope that their children will see a time of complete peace among Jews and all people of the world. Think about the power of thinking such a thought every month!

"Today I'd like to encourage you to compose a יהי רצון of your own. I've used the word 'compose' on purpose because you're not limited to only using words. Sometimes, powerful thoughts and feelings cannot be bound by words. You may wish to compose a song, a *niggun,* or make a sketch. This is an opportunity for you to think about the miraculous changes taking place in your body that, if you choose, will someday allow you to bring life into the world. What kind of world do you want it to be and what can you do to make it that way?"

DICTIONARY DEFINITIONS

Holiness: specially recognized as, or declared sacred by, religious use or authority; consecrated

Infatuation: to inspire or possess with a foolish or unreasoning passion, as of love

Love: (1) the profoundly tender or passionate affection for a person (2) a feeling of warm personal attachment or deep affection, as for a parent, child, or friend (3) sexual passion or desire

Menstruation: The act of periodically discharging blood and mucosal tissue from the uterus, occurring approximately monthly from puberty to menopause

Sacred: (1) devoted or dedicated to a deity or to some religious purpose; consecrated (2) entitled to veneration or religious respect by association with divinity or divine things; holy

HEBREW WORDS AND THEIR ROOTS

קדושה—holiness, separateness

מקווה—ritual bath used monthly by married women, as part of the conversion process, by men in preparation for Shabbat and holidays, by bride and groom before their wedding

אהבה—love

מתנה—gift

כבוד הבריות—respect for all living things

בצלם א-להים—in the image of God

CHALLENGING QUESTIONS THE TEACHER MAY WANT TO RAISE; OR THE GIRLS MAY RAISE

Love and Sex Questions

What's the connection between the physical changes you're beginning to experience and the spiritual ones? How are a person's views about sex and self-esteem connected? How does body image relate to a person's feelings about sex? How does what you see in magazines and on television affect the way you view love and sex? In *The JGirl's Guide* (p. 112), Tamara, age twenty-three, reminisces about her first kiss. She relates a beautiful, respectful interaction. She talks about how private the moment felt to her and that she didn't want to share it with the other girls. It's natural to have intimate feelings for another person and to be attracted to another person. How do you handle those feelings? How do you separate feelings and actions? How do you respond to a boy who's pressuring you to kiss, or touch, or even have sex? What's the relationship between love and sex? Can you have one without the other? What are some of the different types of love you can feel for another person? How do you know when you love someone? What's the difference between love and infatuation? How are holiness and love connected? Can our love for another person help us to love God? Can our love for God help us to love another person? Does it surprise you that so much of the world's literature deals with love and/or sex? What literature dealing with this topic have you read and like the best?

Inquisitive Inquiries

Who can you talk with about the questions you have about sexuality? What do you do if you have a serious question but are uncomfortable speaking about it with another person? Do you think it's helpful to have discussions in groups of girls about sex and love? Small groups? With an adult who can guide you or on your own? Sometimes sexual inappropriateness is subtle and unclear; how do you know if someone is treating you inappropriately? What do you do if someone makes a sexual joke in your presence? How do you handle the spreading of sexual rumors—if you hear them? If you are the target of them? If your friends are the target of them?

THINGS TO THINK ABOUT

You are in the midst of a beautiful and awesome time of change in your body and soul. We live in an age when lots of information is available to us. In addition to reading and learning about the changes you will be experiencing, it's also important to have someone with whom you're comfortable sharing your feelings and questions. Sometimes your mom or dad might be that person, or it might be a teacher, counselor, or older sibling. Don't hesitate to ask questions and to get answers!

OTHER SOURCES

Books/Magazines

Diamant, Anita. *The Red Tent*. New York: St. Martin's Press, 1998. A midrashic novel about the biblical characters of Dinah, Leah and Rachel.

Naylor, Phyllis Reynolds. *Lovingly Alice*. New York: Simon & Schuster, 2004. Fifth grade is tumultuous for Alice as she tries to help others through the many changes occurring at home and in school, including learning about sex when her friend Rosalind gets her period and shares a book that explains what is happening.

————. *Alice on the Outside*. New York: Simon & Schuster, 2000. Eighth-grader Alice has lots of questions about sex, relationships, prejudice, and change.

THINKING BEFORE I SPEAK

Lesson 8

MITZVAH

שמירת הלשון *Shmirat Halashon* (guarding the tongue)

GOALS

To reflect upon our use of language.

To use an important work of American art as a tool for learning to recognize the power of words and to understand that they can be used for good or bad.

To consider the role that facial expressions and body language play in שמירת הלשון.

TEXTS/QUOTES

"'Do not go talebearing among your people' (Leviticus 19:16). This is the commandment against being a gossip. If you have a problem with someone, you should talk to that person, not about the person to someone else" (*The JGirl's Guide,* p. 126).

"Pleasant words are like dripping honey, sweetness for the soul, and health for the bones" (Proverbs 16:24).

"Death and life are in the power of the tongue" (Proverbs 18:21).

PREPARATION

Find a copy of Norman Rockwell's print *The Gossip.* One source is *Norman Rockwell: A Centennial Celebration* (New York: BDD Illustrated Books, 1993). Cover the title of the print until later in the lesson.

BODY OF LESSON

Have the girls sit in a circle and play a round of "Telephone." Teacher: "What just happened? Why was the message we started the game with different from the message that ended the game? Today we're going to focus on the mitzvah of שמירת הלשון, guarding our speech. This is a very difficult mitzvah and one that affects every single one of us every single day. We're going to begin by looking at a print by Norman Rockwell. I've covered up the title because we'll talk about that later. Take some time to look carefully at the print. What do you observe?" (Some possible observations: This painting was done a long time ago; there are pairs of people in conversation; every person in the pairs gets repeated elsewhere in the painting in the next frame, with one exception; different facial expressions—surprise, glee, shock, seriousness, smirking, and anger.) "Observe how Rockwell uses eyes, lips, and hands to tell the story. Let's make a list of all the facial expressions we observe in each pair. What do you think is going on in this painting? What do you think Rockwell was trying to tell us through this painting?

"The name of this painting is *The Gossip*. This word 'gossip' applies to both the person speaking and what the person is saying. Rockwell refers to both meanings in this painting. Can you explain this? Does Rockwell give us a clue as to what the content of the gossip is? Rockwell used his Vermont neighbors in this painting and also included his wife and himself. Why do you think he used so many people instead of just a single pair? Why did he include his wife and himself? How does this painting relate to what happens when we engage in *lashon hara* (literally "evil speech")? Do you think this painting is true to life? Would you have titled the painting *The Gossip* or something else? Although you can't tell from this print, this painting was done in oil on canvas. Would the painting be different if Rockwell had used another medium, such as watercolor or paper cuts? Why or why not?

"This painting tells a story. It is rich with details. This painting is 'read' from left to right, from the top of the page to the bottom. Notice that the first person (upper left corner) and the last person (lower right corner) in the painting are the same woman. Do you think she has learned anything from this experience? Assuming that she has, what would a 'sequel' painting look like? Take the next fifteen minutes to either sketch the sequel or write notes to describe it to someone else in the room. We'll pair up after fifteen minutes to share our sequels. Don't forget to title your artwork!"

DICTIONARY DEFINITIONS

Gossip: (1) idle talk or rumor, especially about the personal or private affairs of others (2) person … given to tattling or idle talk

Silence: (1) absence of any sound or noise; stillness (2) the state or fact of being silent; muteness

Truth: a verified or indisputable fact, proposition, principle or the like

HEBREW WORDS AND THEIR ROOTS

שמירת הלשון—guarding the tongue (watching one's speech)

דבור—speech

אמת—truth

לשון הרע—evil speech

שתיקה—silence

רכילות—gossip

Challenging Questions the Teacher May Want to Raise; Or the Girls May Raise

Language Questions

Are there things that you might say to someone in person that you wouldn't say on the phone or in an e-mail message? Does the way you phrase a comment have an impact on whether or not it's *lashon hara*? What about your facial expression? Your tone of voice? Your body language? The common use of cell phones allows us to communicate from any location. Are there conversations you shouldn't have on your cell phone in the grocery store line? While walking on the street? How does talking on the cell phone affect privacy? Should it affect the types of things about which you speak? E-mail is an open form of communication. Someone you don't know can pick up on an e-mail and use your words. How could this affect *shmirat halashon*?

Inquisitive Inquiries

What do you do when your best friend is speaking *lashon hara* about someone you both know and both don't like? How can you build up your ability to not engage in *lashon hara*? *The JGirl's Guide* (pp. 123–124) lists some examples of *lashon hara:* derogatory statements, damaging statements, insulting statements, emphasizing undesirable traits, belittling statements, and false statements. Reread the examples. Have you ever been the target of *lashon hara*? What did you do? What did others do?

Things to Think About

Watching one's words is a challenging task for *all* people at *all* ages! It takes constant vigilance and self-awareness. How one speaks means being able to put yourself in someone else's shoes. How would it feel if you were on the receiving end of some of the things you say? שמירת הלשון, guarding the tongue, is about recognizing what tremendous power you have to make positive changes in the world, your community, and yourself just by the words you choose!

Other Sources

Books/Magazines

Bayer, Steven. *Wounding with Words* (instant lesson). Los Angeles: Torah Aura Productions, 1996. This instant lesson can be a springboard for the teacher's own creative lesson or be used as is.

Bernstein, David. *Apples of Gold: The Art of Pure Speech*. New York: Torah U'Mesorah Publishing, 1988. The teacher may find some helpful ideas and exercises in this book.

LaFaye, Alexandria. *The Year of the Sawdust Man*. New York: Simon & Schuster, 1998. This book is set in 1934 and focuses on eleven-year-old Nissa as she tries to cope with the gossip in her small Louisiana town when her mother leaves her and her father.

GETTING INVOLVED

MITZVOT

תקון עולם *Tikkun olam* (repairing the world); כל ישראל ערבים זת בזה *Kol Israel areivim zeh bazeh* (all of Israel [all Jews] are responsible for one another)

GOALS

To share with the girls various types of volunteer work available both within the Jewish community and outside it.

To encourage the development of the girls' sensitivity to the needs of others.

To educate the girls about opportunities to apply their unique gifts to enrich the world.

TEXTS/QUOTES

כל ישראל ערבים זת בזה "All of Israel [all Jews] are responsible for one another" (*Sanhedrin* 27b).

לא עליך המלאכה לגמור ולא אתה בן חורין להבטל ממנה "It is not your duty to complete the work, but neither are you free to desist from it" (*Pirkei Avot* 2:21).

"Give to the poor, Jew and non-Jew alike, and thereby bring peace to the world" (*Gitten* 61a).

PREPARATION

Girls' preparation: Either in class or as a preparatory homework assignment, the girls should do the exercise on p. 137 of *The JGirl's Guide* under the "Write" section. Teacher's preparation: Speak with various organizations within the Jewish community (suggestions: senior centers; schools with mentoring programs or that may need help in their office; synagogues; Jewish Federation; Jewish National Fund; Israeli Embassy, for information about projects in Israel), and your larger community (suggestions: parks and recreation department; food pantries; soup kitchens; Big Brothers/Big Sisters; animal shelters; organizations that raise money to find cures for diseases, like March of Dimes). Ask if a representative can come to visit with the girls and if she or he can send/bring literature about the organization. You may wish to stagger the speakers across several sessions or have several speakers on a single day. Be sure to have a mix of speakers from both Jewish and non-Jewish organizations. It's important for the girls to recognize that they are members of a Jewish community as well as a world community. It is our obligation to be actively involved in both arenas.

BODY OF LESSON

Begin the lesson by having each girl make a paper doll chain. Once each girl has a row of dolls, point out that they are connected by their hands and feet. Share with them that this is a metaphor for being a part of a community. Each of us has our own identity and special gifts and talents, but we are part of a bigger whole. We need to share our talents with our community just as we benefit from the talents of others.

Teacher: "Today we're going to learn about some of the opportunities that exist in our community for volunteer work and do some reflecting on how we can get involved and make a difference. Before we hear from some of the speakers I'd like you to look at the exercise you completed before class. You wrote down the problems you'd like to fix within our world, country, the Jewish people, and personally. These ideas should be uppermost in your mind as you listen to the speakers because you may learn of an opportunity to begin תקון עולם today! Please put the paper doll chains aside because we'll be using them at the end of the lesson."

After the presentations the teacher will share the following with the girls: "You've been given a lot of information today and there's a lot to digest and think about. Take a few minutes to write on your doll chains. You may want to write the names of some organizations you're interested in helping. You may want to write some questions you have, or some thoughts that occurred to you during the presentations."

DICTIONARY DEFINITIONS

Balance: (1) state of equilibrium or equipoise; equal distribution of weight, amount, etc. (2) mental steadiness or emotional stability; habit of calm behavior, judgment

Charity: (1) charitable actions as almsgiving or performing other benevolent actions of any sort for the needy with no expectation of material reward (2) something given to a person or persons in need

Justice: the quality of being just; righteousness, equitableness or moral rightness

Pollute: to make foul or unclean; dirty

Poverty: (1) the state or condition of having little or no money, goods or means of support; condition of being poor (2) scantiness; insufficiency

Righteousness: the quality or state of being just or rightful

Terrorism: the state of fear and submission so produced

HEBREW WORDS AND THEIR ROOTS

איזון—balance

סביבה—environment

חסד—kindness

הלבשת ערומים—clothing the naked

צדק—righteousness, justice

צדקה—charity

תקון עולם—repairing the world

CHALLENGING QUESTIONS THE TEACHER MAY WANT TO RAISE; OR THE GIRLS MAY RAISE

Leadership Questions

Reread the story about Moses's and Jethro's flock (*The JGirl's Guide,* p. 138). In this story, the Torah tells us some of Moses's qualities. What were they? Why would they be important qualities for a leader to have? In Chapter 2 of *The JGirl's Guide* you read about Rebecca. What were the qualities she possessed? Why are they important qualities for a leader to have? If you were to list qualities that should be exhibited by a leader, what would they be? How can every person be a leader? When have you served as a leader in your family? Your school? Your synagogue? Your community? How does getting involved in your community make you a leader? Do you think it is important for Jews to volunteer in non-Jewish organizations? Similarly, do you think non-Jews should volunteer in Jewish organizations? Why or why not?

Inquisitive Inquiries

Imagine that everyone in your community was a musical instrument in an orchestra. Every instrument has to play well individually and as a member of the orchestra. Using this metaphor, discuss how you can repair the world. How can you become more sensitive to the plight of others? What kinds of repair work do you do on a regular basis? Taking the phrase כל ישראל ערבים זת בזה seriously isn't always an easy thing, particularly since we don't always agree with one another. What does being responsible for another person mean to you? Is sacrifice involved? What should you expect as a volunteer? What do you do if the person you are trying to help doesn't show up? What do you do if you discover problems you didn't know about in advance? Alexis de Tocqueville, a Frenchman who studied America in the 1830s, said that one of the unusual characteristics of American society is that we volunteer and we create volunteer organizations. Why do you think Americans do that, perhaps more than other people?

THINGS TO THINK ABOUT

No one else in the entire world can fill the role that you can. Each of us has unique talents that will help this world become a kinder, more beautiful place in which all of us can live. We have an obligation to discover what our special gifts are and find ways to develop them and use them. The first place to start with תקון עולם is with ourselves. Who can be a resource in helping you uncover your gifts? What kinds of things can you do yourself to discover your gifts? Spend some time in the coming weeks thinking about the answers to these questions. Many people ignore their own talents. Other people exaggerate their abilities. You don't have to do either.

OTHER SOURCES

Books/Magazines

Grishaver, Joel Lurie, and Beth Huppin. *Tzedakah, Gemilut Chasadim and Ahavah: A Manual for World Repair.* Denver: ARE Publishing, 1983. This activity-based book contains texts and focuses on *mitzvot* such as freeing captives, visiting the sick, giving loans, and *tzedakah.*

Shavit Artson, Bradley. *It's a Mitzvah: Step-by-Step to Jewish Living.* Springfield, NJ: Behrman House, 1995. Explores *mitzvot,* with photographs.

Siegel, Danny. *Munbaz II and Other Mitzvah Heroes.* Pittsboro, NC: The Town House Press, 1994. Presents stories about people who are "mitzvah heroes." A great resource to show students how regular people, including children, can make a difference in the world.

———. *1 + 1 = 3 And 37 Other Mitzvah Properties to Live By.* Pittsboro, NC: The Town House Press, 2000. Includes phone numbers, e-mail addresses, and websites to directly contact people from *Munbaz.*

Websites

www.ziv.org—Danny Siegel's website. There are lots of hands-on *tikkun olam* activities at this site.

BECOMING MYSELF

MITZVOT

בת מצוה *Bat mitzvah* (becoming a Jewish woman); תלמוד תורה *Talmud Torah* (Torah study)

GOALS

To provide the girls with an opportunity for deep reflection about their Jewish identity.

To encourage them, if appropriate, to embrace a new meaning of being a bat mitzvah.

TEXTS/QUOTES

"These are things whose fruits a person eats in this world, while in the world to come a person will reap even more: honoring parents, deeds of lovingkindness, going to the house of study morning and evening, hospitality to guests, visiting the sick, attending a bride, burying the dead, meaningful prayer, making peace between people; but the study of Torah exceeds them all" (*Shabbat* 127a).

שמצוה גוררת מצוה "For one mitzvah leads to another mitzvah" (*Mishna Avot* 4:2).

הפך בה והפך בה דכלה בה "Turn it and turn it, for everything is in it" (*Pirkei Avot* 5:26).

PREPARATION

Find different types of *talitot* to bring to class. Look for *talitot* that are different sizes and fabrics, *talitot* with different *atarot,* different colored stripes, and hand-painted ones. Bring these to class for the opening of the lesson. Ask the girls in advance to bring a white t-shirt to class (you may wish to have a few on hand in case someone forgets hers). Have decorative materials such as markers, puffy glue, tissue paper, construction paper, scissors, newspapers, magazines. Have blank CDs or cassette tapes with a CD/tape recorder in the room.

At some point before or during the lesson, the teacher should make clear that talking about the *talit* as a "kind of Jewish *tefillah* uniform" does not mean that one can pray only while wearing a *talit*. Some girls wear a *talit* and some do not. There are girls who wear *talitot* but only at their bat mitzvah or when they are on the *bimah*. There are varying practices within Judaism over this issue. Frequently the *talitot* girls have are decorated with flowers and colors. What's essential about the *talit* is the number of *tzizit* (fringes) and how they are knotted.

Assign the "Write" section on p. 160 of *The JGirl's Guide* as a homework assignment. Let the girls know they will be using this assignment for a project in class at the next session. It is possible that this lesson may have to be completed over more than a single session. If you have the flexibility to do the entire lesson in one longer session that would be preferable.

BODY OF LESSON

Teacher: "Today I've brought in lots of different types of *talitot*. What do you observe about these *talitot*? What is the same in all of the *talitot* (צִיצִית—*tzizit*)? The *talit* is a kind of Jewish *tefillah* uniform. What is the purpose of a uniform?" (To identify yourself as part of a group/community. You might get other answers such as to be constricting, block your creativity; encourage that conversation, and then bring the discussion back to the first answer.) "What other types of uniforms can you name?" (Sports, orchestra, marching band, business suits, popular clothing.) "In sports everyone on the team might have the same color jersey, but what's different about each one?" (The number, the person wearing it.)

"The reason I brought in these *talitot* is that I want us to consider the idea of Jewish identity. You have written some responses to the questions on p. 160 of *The JGirl's Guide*. These questions were posed to help you think about Jewish identity. Let's break into groups of three and share some of our answers to those questions." The teacher should circulate among the groups.

After the girls have had sufficient time to share, the teacher should move to the next phase of the lesson. "Even if a person is wearing a uniform they still remain an individual with an important role to play. Each of us is unique, but what we have in common is that we are all Jewish. We're going to be creating a 'Jewish uniform' today using the t-shirts you brought in. Each uniform will be unique because you will put your own special mark on your uniform. You'll be using the answers to your questions and translating those answers into an art form. For example, let's say you identify strongly with Israel. You might represent that on your t-shirt with a depiction of the shape of the State of Israel or an icon representing a site in Israel.

"Before we individualize our uniforms, we have to think about what is going to be common to all the uniforms. Remember, every *talit* we looked at was a little different, but what they all had in common was the צִיצִית, *tzizit*. We're going to have a whole-class discussion now about what we're going to do to the t-shirts to represent what we all have in common as Jews. What do you think is the common element(s) that *all* Jews need to have in order to be called Jewish?" Jews argue about this all the time. As "almost adults" the girls can now become part of this conversation. Their views are important. They represent the next generation.

The teacher should anticipate that this might be a very heated conversation among the girls. Set expectations before the conversation about respectful communication. Help facilitate the conversation until the girls reach a decision. You may wish to discuss with the girls in advance how they'll decide what the common element(s) will be (will everyone have to agree, or will you go with the majority?). Once a decision is reached, the girls should be given the opportunity to create their t-shirts. Remind them that in addition to the visual arts, they may wish to add an auditory component to their uniform. For example, the girls might decide that the *Shema* is a declaration common to all Jews. That could be done as an audio tape with everyone singing or saying the words. Let them know that CDs or cassettes are available for that purpose.

As a means of closure you may wish to have the girls share their t-shirts with one another, explaining what aspects of Jewish identity they have represented on their t-shirt.

DICTIONARY DEFINITIONS

Identity: (1) state or fact of remaining the same one, as under varying aspects or conditions (2) condition or character as to who a person or what a thing is

Jew: (1) a person whose religion is Judaism (2) one of a scattered group of people that traces its descent from the biblical Hebrews

Model: (1) a standard or example for imitation or comparison (2) worthy to serve as a model; exemplary

Uniform: (1) having a single form or pattern; consistently following a definite formula or set of rules (2) a distinctive style or fashion of dress; a uniform design or characteristic pattern of clothing which identifies members of a group or organization (3) a single suit or outfit of a uniform style

HEBREW WORDS AND THEIR ROOTS

דבר תורה—literally "words of Torah," a speech given using citations from Torah

הפטרה—Haftarah, reading from the prophets, from the word הפטיר, to conclude

שהחינו—blessing said over something new

בית מדרש—house of study

הלכה—literally "the way," Jewish law

עם ישראל—the People of Israel

חברותא—learning partner, from the word חבר, friend

ישיבה—a school for Torah study

אושפיזין—special guests from Jewish history whom we invite to our sukkah

טלית—prayer shawl

ציצת—fringes

CHALLENGING QUESTIONS THE TEACHER MAY WANT TO RAISE; OR THE GIRLS MAY RAISE

Identity Questions

What are the elements of a Jewish identity that make it different from a non-Jewish identity? How do you define your Jewish identity? Are there things you do that are specifically Jewish? Are there things you do that aren't specifically Jewish, but the way you do them defines you as a Jew? If you met a girl who was planning to convert to Judaism, what would you say are the key elements of being a JGirl?

How does sharing a common language frame Jewish identity? What about sharing common customs? Can non-Jewish women and men be role models to help define your Jewish identity? Jews come from a multitude of backgrounds and identify themselves as Jews in different ways. Do you think there are certain common elements that all Jews must have in order to be called Jewish? What might those elements be? Jews are an unusual ancient people in that we've maintained our Jewish identity for centuries, much of that time outside of the Land of Israel. Why do you think we've survived as a people without being attached to a country?

Inquisitive Inquiries

Since, unlike in generations of the past, it's easy to blend in and not advertise your Jewishness, do you think it's easier or harder to be a Jew in America today? Who are your Jewish role models? What are the qualities they possess? Do you think you are a Jewish role model for others?

THINGS TO THINK ABOUT

We live in a time of tremendous freedom both as Jews and as women. We can be and do almost anything we want. That makes it even more important for us to think about our Jewish identity. Our identities will evolve and develop over the years and becoming a bat mitzvah is just the beginning of that journey. Take time to read, think, and visit with people as you begin to shape your Jewish identity. You will have many questions. That's normal and healthy! Seek out Jewish women who are older, learn their stories, and incorporate their experiences into your own. You are a link in a chain of Jewish women that spans thousands of years from the past and into the future.

OTHER SOURCES

Books/Magazines

Bush, Lawrence. *Emma Ansky-Levine and Her Mitzvah Machine.* New York: URJ Press, 1998. For her twelfth birthday, Emma receives a special Mitzvah Machine that helps her discover her Jewish identity and the true meaning of becoming a bat mitzvah.

Feinstein, Edward. *Tough Questions Jews Ask: A Young Adult's Guide to Building a Jewish Life.* Woodstock, Vt.: Jewish Lights, 2003. A great read for all ages.

Freeman, Susan. *Teaching Jewish Virtues: Sacred Sources and Art Activities.* Denver: ARE Publishing, 1999. This book features text study and activities.

Grishaver, Joel Lurie. *40 Things You Can Do to Save the Jewish People: Parenting Tips for Raising "Good Enough" Jewish Kids.* Los Angeles: Aleph Design Group, 1997. This excellent resource contains suggestions, stories, activities, and many thought-provoking ideas.

Isaacs, Ronald H., and Kerry M. Olitzky. *Doing Mitzvot: Mitzvah Projects for Bar/Bat Mitzvah.* Jersey City: KTAV, 1994. Written for children in their bat/bar mitzvah year, this book introduces the practice of *mitzvot. Mitzvot* are offered for every month and there are suggested projects. There is also a list of organizations children might be interested in helping.

Pearl, Judea and Ruth, eds. *I Am Jewish: Personal Reflections Inspired by the Last Words of Daniel Pearl.* Woodstock, Vt.: Jewish Lights, 2005. Over 147 people reflect upon what it means to them when they say, "I am Jewish."

Salkin, Jeffrey K. *For Kids—Putting God On Your Guest List: How to Claim the Spiritual Meaning of Your Bar/Bat Mitzvah.* Woodstock, Vt.: Jewish Lights,1998. An important resource to help kids spiritually prepare for their bat/bar mitzvah.

Sandberg, Martin I. *Tefillin.* New York: United Synagogue of Conservative Judaism, 1992. The first chapter discusses how *tefillin* is a type of Jewish uniform.

Siegel, Danny. *The Bar and Bat Mitzvah* Mitzvah *Book: A Practical Guide for Changing the World through Your Simcha.* Pittsboro, NC: The Town House Press, 2004. This book does what the title says. It gives practical assistance about speech writing, mitzvah opportunities, and mitzvah projects.

Wolff, Ferida. *Pink Slippers, Bat Mitzvah Blues.* Philadelphia: Jewish Publication Society, 1994. Thirteen-year-old Alyssa tries to balance the conflicting demands of ballet training with finding her place as a Jew in today's world.

Movies

Yentl, directed by Barbra Streisand. Los Angeles: MGM Studios, 1989. At the beginning of the movie there is a scene which shows Yentl (Barbra Streisand) putting on a *talit.* This brief scene shot in candlelight demonstrates Yentl's spiritual connection with God, prayer, and ritual. It might be an interesting piece to show at the start of the lesson and engage the girls in conversation.

About Jewish Lights

People of all faiths and backgrounds yearn for books that attract, engage, educate, and spiritually inspire.

Our principal goal is to stimulate thought and help all people learn about who the Jewish People are, where they come from, and what the future can be made to hold. While people of our diverse Jewish heritage are the primary audience, our books speak to people in the Christian world as well and will broaden their understanding of Judaism and the roots of their own faith.

We bring to you authors who are at the forefront of spiritual thought and experience. While each has something different to say, they all say it in a voice that you can hear.

Our books are designed to welcome you and then to engage, stimulate, and inspire. We judge our success not only by whether or not our books are beautiful and commercially successful, but by whether or not they make a difference in your life.

For a complete list of all Jewish Lights books, request our catalog by calling us at (800) 962-4544, faxing to (802) 457-4004, or view it online at www.jewishlights.com.

Stuart M. Matlins, Publisher

The Book of Miracles AWARD WINNER!
A Young Person's Guide to Jewish Spiritual Awareness
by Lawrence Kushner

For ages 9 & up

Introduces kids to a way of everyday spiritual thinking to last a lifetime. Kushner, whose award-winning books have brought spirituality to life for countless adults, now shows young people how to use Judaism as a foundation on which to build their lives.
6 x 9, 96 pp, HC, 2-color illus., ISBN 1-879045-78-8 **$16.95**

For Kids—Putting God on Your Guest List
How to Claim the Spiritual Meaning of Your Bar or Bat Mitzvah
by Rabbi Jeffrey K. Salkin

For ages 11–12

An important resource for kids ages 11 and 12, to help them spiritually prepare for their bar/bat mitzvah.

Salkin instructs, engages and inspires in a language young people can understand to teach the core spiritual values of Judaism. Discussion questions at the end of each chapter give them the opportunity to engage with the text, process what they have learned, and offer their own thoughts.
6 x 9, 144 pp, Quality Paperback ISBN 1-58023-015-6 **$14.95**

The Story of the Jews
A 4,000-Year Adventure—A Graphic History Book
Written and illustrated by *Stan Mack*

For all ages

Through witty cartoons and accurate narrative, illustrates the major characters and events that have shaped the Jewish people and culture.
6 x 9, 304 pp, Quality PB, Illus., ISBN 1-58023-155-1 **$16.95**

The Triumph of Eve & Other Subversive Bible Tales
by Matt Biers-Ariel

For ages 13 & up

Many people were taught and remember only a one-dimensional Bible. These engaging retellings are the antidote to this—they're witty, often hilarious, always profound, and invite you to grapple with questions and issues that are often hidden in the original text.
5½ x 8½, 192 pp, HC, ISBN 1-59473-040-7 **$19.99**

Also Available: **The Triumph of Eve Teacher's Guide**
8½ x 11, 48 pp (est), PB, ISBN 1-59473-152-7 **$8.99**

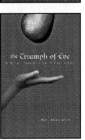

Holidays/Holy Days

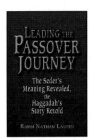

Leading the Passover Journey
The Seder's Meaning Revealed, the Haggadah's Story Retold
By Rabbi Nathan Laufer
Uncovers the hidden meaning of the Seder's rituals and customs.
6 x 9, 208 pp, Hardcover, ISBN 1-58023-211-6 **$24.99**

Reclaiming Judaism as a Spiritual Practice
Holy Days and Shabbat
By Rabbi Goldie Milgram
Provides a framework for understanding the powerful and often unexplained intellectual, emotional, and spiritual tools that are essential for a lively, relevant, and fulfilling Jewish spiritual practice. 7 x 9, 272 pp, Quality PB, ISBN 1-58023-205-1 **$19.99**

7th Heaven
Celebrating Shabbat with Rebbe Nachman of Breslov
By Moshe Mykoff with the Breslov Research Institute
Explores the art of consciously observing Shabbat and understanding in-depth many of the day's spiritual practices. 5⅛ x 8¼, 224 pp, Deluxe PB w/flaps, ISBN 1-58023-175-6 **$18.95**

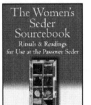

The Women's Passover Companion
Women's Reflections on the Festival of Freedom
Edited by Rabbi Sharon Cohen Anisfeld, Tara Mohr and Catherine Spector
Groundbreaking. A provocative conversation about women's relationships to Passover as well as the roots and meanings of women's seders.
6 x 9, 352 pp, Hardcover, ISBN 1-58023-128-4 **$24.95**

The Women's Seder Sourcebook
Rituals & Readings for Use at the Passover Seder
Edited by Rabbi Sharon Cohen Anisfeld, Tara Mohr and Catherine Spector
Gathers the voices of more than one hundred women in readings, personal and creative reflections, commentaries, blessings, and ritual suggestions that can be incorporated into your Passover celebration. 6 x 9, 384 pp, Hardcover, ISBN 1-58023-136-5 **$24.95**

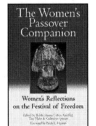

Creating Lively Passover Seders: *A Sourcebook of Engaging Tales, Texts & Activities*
By David Arnow, Ph.D. 7 x 9, 416 pp, Quality PB, ISBN 1-58023-184-5 **$24.99**

Hanukkah, 2nd Edition: *The Family Guide to Spiritual Celebration*
By Dr. Ron Wolfson. Edited by Joel Lurie Grishaver.
7 x 9, 240 pp, illus., Quality PB, ISBN 1-58023-122-5 **$18.95**

The Jewish Family Fun Book: *Holiday Projects, Everyday Activities, and Travel Ideas with Jewish Themes* By Danielle Dardashti and Roni Sarig. Illus. by Avi Katz.
6 x 9, 288 pp, 70+ b/w illus. & diagrams, Quality PB, ISBN 1-58023-171-3 **$18.95**

The Jewish Gardening Cookbook: *Growing Plants & Cooking for Holidays & Festivals*
By Michael Brown 6 x 9, 224 pp, 30+ illus., Quality PB, ISBN 1-58023-116-0 **$16.95**

The Jewish Lights Book of Fun Classroom Activities: *Simple and Seasonal Projects for Teachers and Students* By Danielle Dardashti and Roni Sarig
6 x 9, 240 pp, Quality PB, ISBN 1–58023–206–X **$19.99**

Passover, 2nd Edition: *The Family Guide to Spiritual Celebration*
By Dr. Ron Wolfson with Joel Lurie Grishaver
7 x 9, 352 pp, Quality PB, ISBN 1-58023-174-8 **$19.95**

Shabbat, 2nd Edition: *The Family Guide to Preparing for and Celebrating the Sabbath*
By Dr. Ron Wolfson 7 x 9, 320 pp, illus., Quality PB, ISBN 1-58023-164-0 **$19.95**

Sharing Blessings: *Children's Stories for Exploring the Spirit of the Jewish Holidays*
By Rahel Musleah and Michael Klayman
8½ x 11, 64 pp, Full-color illus., Hardcover, ISBN 1-879045-71-0 **$18.95**
For ages 6 & up

Bar/Bat Mitzvah

Tough Questions Jews Ask: *A Young Adult's Guide to Building a Jewish Life*
By Rabbi Edward Feinstein
Invites you to explore the difficult questions that are central to Jewish religious and spiritual life, and welcomes you to join the discussion that has helped shape what Judaism is today—and can be—in the future.
6 x 9, 160 pp, Quality PB, ISBN 1-58023-139-X **$14.99** For ages 13 & up
    Also Available: **Tough Questions Jews Ask Teacher's Guide**
    8½ x 11, 72 pp, PB, ISBN 1-58023-187-X **$8.95**

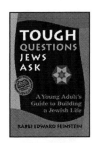

Bar/Bat Mitzvah Basics: *A Practical Family Guide to Coming of Age Together*
    By Helen Leneman 6 x 9, 240 pp, Quality PB, ISBN 1-58023-151-9 **$18.95**

The Bar/Bat Mitzvah Memory Book: *An Album for Treasuring the Spiritual Celebration*
    By Rabbi Jeffrey K. Salkin and Nina Salkin
    8 x 10, 48 pp, Deluxe Hardcover, 2-color text, ribbon marker, ISBN 1-58023-111-X **$19.95**

For Kids—Putting God on Your Guest List: *How to Claim the Spiritual Meaning of Your Bar or Bat Mitzvah* *By Rabbi Jeffrey K. Salkin*
    6 x 9, 144 pp, Quality PB, ISBN 1-58023-015-6 **$14.99** For ages 11–12

Putting God on the Guest List, 3rd Edition: *How to Reclaim the Spiritual Meaning of Your Child's Bar or Bat Mitzvah* *By Rabbi Jeffrey K. Salkin*
    6 x 9, 224 pp, Quality PB, ISBN 1-58023-222-1 **$16.99**; Hardcover, ISBN 1-58023-260-4 **$24.99**
    Also Available: **Putting God on the Guest List Teacher's Guide**
    8½ x 11, 48 pp (est), PB, ISBN 1-58023-226-4 **$8.99**

Spirituality/Women's Interest

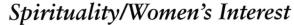

The Quotable Jewish Woman: *Wisdom, Inspiration & Humor from the Mind & Heart* *Edited and compiled by Elaine Bernstein Partnow*
The definitive collection of ideas, reflections, humor, and wit of over 300 Jewish women.
6 x 9, 496 pp, Hardcover, ISBN 1-58023-193-4 **$29.99**

Lifecycles, Vol. 1: *Jewish Women on Life Passages & Personal Milestones*
    Edited and with introductions by Rabbi Debra Orenstein 6 x 9, 480 pp, Quality PB,
    ISBN 1-58023-018-0 **$19.95**

Lifecycles, Vol. 2: *Jewish Women on Biblical Themes in Contemporary Life*
    Edited and with introductions by Rabbi Debra Orenstein and Rabbi Jane Rachel Litman
    6 x 9, 464 pp, Quality PB, ISBN 1-58023-019-9 **$19.95**

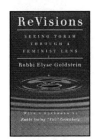

Moonbeams: *A Hadassah Rosh Hodesh Guide* *Edited by Carol Diament, Ph.D.*
    8½ x 11, 240 pp, Quality PB, ISBN 1-58023-099-7 **$20.00**

ReVisions: *Seeing Torah through a Feminist Lens* *By Rabbi Elyse Goldstein*
    5½ x 8½, 224 pp, Quality PB, ISBN 1-58023-117-9 **$16.95**

Women of the Wall: *Claiming Sacred Ground at Judaism's Holy Site*
    Edited by Phyllis Chesler and Rivka Haut
    6 x 9, 496 pp, b/w photos, Hardcover, ISBN 1-58023-161-6 **$34.95**

The Women's Haftarah Commentary: *New Insights from Women Rabbis on the 54 Weekly Haftarah Portions, the 5 Megillot & Special Shabbatot*
    Edited by Rabbi Elyse Goldstein 6 x 9, 560 pp, Hardcover, ISBN 1-58023-133-0 **$39.99**

The Women's Torah Commentary: *New Insights from Women Rabbis on the 54 Weekly Torah Portions* *Edited by Rabbi Elyse Goldstein*
    6 x 9, 496 pp, Hardcover, ISBN 1-58023-076-8 **$34.95**

The Year Mom Got Religion: *One Woman's Midlife Journey into Judaism*
    By Lee Meyerhoff Hendler 6 x 9, 208 pp, Quality PB, ISBN 1-58023-070-9 **$15.95**

I Am Jewish: *Personal Reflections Inspired by the Last Words of Daniel Pearl*
Almost 150 Jews—both famous and not—from all walks of life, from all around the world, write about Identity, Heritage, Covenant / Chosenness and Faith, Humanity and Ethnicity, and *Tikkun Olam* and Justice. *Edited by Judea and Ruth Pearl*
6 x 9, 304 pp, Deluxe PB w/flaps, ISBN 1-58023-259-0 **$18.99**; Hardcover, ISBN 1-58023-183-7 **$24.99**
Download a free copy of the *I Am Jewish Teacher's Guide* at our website: www.jewishlights.com